Towards

Success

Become a Successful Professional

Life is a game. Play it well for your own good.

*A proper balancing of the emotional, physical as
well as physiological aspects of your life
can help you find your place
anywhere under the sun.*

GEORGE MALIAKAL

This edition is published in 2017 by

GLAN BOOKS,

21 Uma Nagar, Thrissur – 680655, Kerala, India.

E-mail : glan221045@gmail.com

ISBN: 9781549647383

Price

Dedicated
To
My Family

Table of Contents

Interview

What is an Interview? Type of Interviews – What makes a good Interview? – Why preparation so important? – How do you present yourself? – Anxious moments while waiting – At the Interview – Interview for a Change of Job – Some likely Questions at the Interview – Why many people don't make the grade at the Interview? – Some Helpful Tips.

New Work Culture

Work Culture – Company Culture - The Structure – Job Satisfaction – The Relationship – Be Professional and Effective – Take on What You can Chew – No Gossiping – Keep Open Your Communication Channels – Good Communication Skill.

Work Culture in Information Technology

The Structure – Skill and Knowledge – Job Satisfaction – Working Environment – Supervision – Promotion – Perform or Quit – Stock Options – Profit Sharing Plan – Frequent Change of Companies – The Guiding Principle.

Careers in IT- Risk Factors

Work Pressure – An Unpredictable Profession – Your Personal Qualities Can Make or Break Your Career – Losing Interest over a Period of Time – Job Security.

Search for your Dream Job

Job Search – Why Go Online? - Job Search – Before You Go Online - Select the Right Sites for your Job Search - New to Job Search? Tips for finding your Dream Job.

How to become a Successful Professional

Some tips – Developing your Skills - Building Professional Relationship – Taking Control of your Profession.

Final Tips: The secrets

Preface

At the outset, let me tell you, 'Why I wrote this book, titled "Towards Success"? And I had many reasons.

Writing is a Passion for me. Whether, while I was in the army or even after my premature retirement after 20 years, in spite of my hectic activities, I always used to find time to write on any topics that came to my mind. The rich life experience I had throughout my life, also gave me lot of inspiration for writing.

My recent blog topics on 'Job Search' have been my favorite topics to help people searching for some jobs and help them to build up a good career for themselves.

"Towards Success- Become A Successful Professional", my recent book, is an 'All in One solution' for the Personal and Career Growth of young and old alike. It explains everything that you need to develop and practice as you grow, till you attain your goal of becoming a Successful Professional.

This reference book will help you to find your Dream Jobs and also help you to 'groom' to become a Successful Professional in their career.

But, remember, you cannot realize your Dreams unless you work hard to realize your dreams. And such a dream of becoming a Successful Professional doesn't happen overnight. For this, we have to plan, plan from the very beginning and it starts from your 'Childhood'.

Developing your 'Personal and Leadership' qualities and building up a good 'Personality' are all very important. It is true, your parents and family members and friends can certainly help you in your endeavor. But it is your interest and hard work that matters.

The content of this reference book, also includes all the latest 'thought process' like, 'New Work Culture', the need for a good 'Inter Personal Skill and a Good Communication skill, that will help you to attain your goal.

I am quite certain, this will be one of the 'most sought after reference book' for you and others in your family, as a source of inspiration and guide.

With the recent invention of 'text to read' App, now you can very comfortably listen to this book using the Kindle Text Reader App, like an audio book. I have listened to the content many a times and found very interesting. By this way, you can listen to any part of the content whenever you wish to, making it very easy for you.

George Maliakal
Author

The Beginning

I still remember, years back, once I was giving a talk to the Higher Secondary School students on Personality Development and Career Opportunities. I began with a simple question.

"You have to select the 'Best Student' of your school, how will you go about selecting the 'Best Student'? I asked.

"By evaluating their overall performance"; with a loud voice they answered. There wasn't any difference of opinion.

'Thus, ideally you will select a student, who has the *highest score in academics*, who is *good in extra-curricular activities*, who has a *good character and behavior* and who also *possesses leadership qualities*, no?' I again asked.

'Yes.' Once again they confirmed their earlier answer. But they were not very clear about the leadership qualities. They gave a blank look. I knew their mind and I continued.

'So, if you want to become the 'Best Student' of your school, it is 'YOU' who should work for it. And your parents, teachers and friends will help you and give full support in your efforts.'

'But you know very well that there is only one 'Best Student' in a school. So what is the point in putting such a major effort for such a difficult selection? This must be worrying your mind.' I asked them. As I paused for a while I looked into their eyes. They all had something in their mind for me but were unable to express.

I continued, 'We all know that every student cannot become the 'Best Student' of the school. But you all can become 'Good Students' of your school, no?'

'Yes.' Once again, they answered loud and clear with a big smile.

And that was the beginning of my talk to them on 'Personality Development'.

Children going to school know about various individual qualities as given in their progress cards. The qualities only varied little from school to school. They also knew well that such personal qualities were graded at the end of each term and they were part of their overall grading system. Even children at the school level know that for being chosen as the best student of the lot they need to have academic excellence and good personal qualities.

But they never paid any particular attention to those personal qualities nor did they make any known effort to realise the values of such personal qualities and improve them in their personal lives. They took them for granted as they possessed them and they grew along with them until they started hearing about 'Character Formation' and 'Personality Development'.

By the way, when and where do you begin to learn about all those personal qualities? And what are those personal qualities?

You begin to learn about these personal qualities from your own homes, from your parents and from other members of your family. And you begin to learn from such a young age.

As you start understanding about things and as you start registering things in your mind, your learning process starts and you also start developing your personal qualities slowly.

As you grow, you start going to the school. At school you interact with many children coming from different family background, different places and from different environment and thus you get a greater opportunity to learn and develop various personal qualities from other students of your school.

And what are those Personal Qualities? I asked them again.

I wanted to know from them about various personal qualities that are given in their School Progress Cards, which they were well aware from their school progress cards.

They said a number of them. But they were incomplete and were in a random order.

Therefore, I summarized them: *neat and tidy, punctuality, self-confidence, determination, sincere, hardworking, active, honest, trustworthy, willing, responsible, co-operation, self-discipline, sportsman-spirit, cheerful, shyness, aggressive, rigid, shrewd etc.*

Personal Qualities

There are a number of 'Personal Qualities' that we want our children to learn and possess in their life as they grow. And as children start going to school they learn more about them. And our guidance and timely help make a lot of difference.

Neat and Tidy

You need to wear clean cloths and wear them properly. Everybody knows that you cannot afford to wear new dress every time. But whatever you have, you must wear it clean. It also includes the footwear if you have any. It will give an impression to others that you are very conscious about your personal hygiene and your interest in creating a good impression in others.

It is also important while you are studying in a school where you mingle with hundreds of students coming from different places and environments.

Punctuality

It's a quality you develop immediately after you start coming to the school like coming to school at the right time, to be in your class in time, getting back to the class after various intervals, to be there at the given time where your teacher wants you to assemble, reporting on time for various other activities, meeting your friends at the given time and place etc.

Though initially you may feel as if it has been thrust upon you, gradually you start realizing its importance in your life. It's something that we expect from others or rather expect others to follow.

Self-confidence

It's having confidence in oneself, a feeling of certainty, a trust in one's own ability. It's a feeling you generate after identifying your abilities and potential that you can do or that you can accomplish the task ahead of you. 'This? Oh! This I can do it.' That kind of a strong feeling coming from within yourself helps you to proceed confidently and do well in your studies as well as in other activities.

Self-confidence is something you generate within yourself, over the period as you grow up in your life. Little things that you accomplish in your day to day life add to your confidence. It's quite an essential personal quality for the success in your life.

Determination

It's a strong desire to do a thing. Rather it is your strong *Will* to achieve anything that you are confident to achieve. Like say you are coming to school to gain knowledge and score a high grading and you are confident that you can achieve them. Now you have a strong will to achieve them, which makes you physically work till you achieve your goal. And that is determination.

Sincere

It is your natural and genuine behavior. You want to do something and you put in your true efforts with an aim of achieving the same, like you are coming to school to learn, gain knowledge and to score a high grading. So you try to put in your best. It's yet another good personal quality, being sincere to self and you must also be very sincere to your friends, teachers, parents and others, in your words and deeds.

Hardworking

Hard work is the key to success and there is no shortcut to hard work. It is as simple as that. Anything that you want to achieve in your life, you need to put your mental and physical efforts as the situation demands. And your efforts must be sincere. Only then you shall achieve the desired results.

At schools/ colleges you need to put in your mental and physical efforts to learn and the result depends on the handwork you put in. If you work harder you get a better result.

At times you may find things little difficult that you thought it to be. But never give up. Work hard and work harder till you achieve the desired result. A sense of achievement will boost your self-confidence.

Active

It means being active both mentally and physically. Both are required to make you as an active person. You need to maintain a healthy body and a healthy mind. This will help you in your thinking, your words and your actions, which will have a great bearing on your personal as well as professional life.

You often find some people who are really slow and at the same time some are really very fast. Your effort should be to achieve a reasonable speed both in your thoughts and actions. That's the only way you can manage more things in a short period of time.

Honest

It is one of the important qualities your parents try to teach you even as a small child – to tell the truth always and nothing but the truth. Little things you do at home, your parents' guide you and correct you when you go wrong.

At schools and colleges you get ample opportunities to develop this quality and to test yourself about your honesty. By being honest, your mind will always be free of tension, which will help you to fully concentrate in your activities; whereas if you are dishonest you shall be always under tension which will definitely affect your personal and professional life.

Trustworthy

It's a feeling that you create in others that they can trust you, building their confidence in you. Mostly you start realizing its effect at your schools and colleges where other students start trusting you. And at times you feel bad to realize that some of them don't trust you.

It all begins from little things that you speak and do over a period. It can be in your personal life, between parents and between other family members. There is also a need to develop a mutual trust among others especially your colleagues.

Willing

It is an interest for doing things. You must have *a will* to learn and *a will* to do. It is a sign of progress. Things should not be forced upon an individual. Whether it is in your home or at your school / college or work place, you must have a will to work. Only then you will feel happy and contented in your work. Only then you will find and get a job satisfaction. There must be a willingness to accept works and a willingness to accept responsibilities.

Responsible

From your childhood you start accepting responsibilities at home, at your school and college and on many other occasions. It adds sincerity to what you do and inspiration to do well. Because you know that you will be held responsible for your actions especially if anything goes wrong. This will help others in grading you as a person who can be relied upon or as a person who can be depended upon.

Co-operation

It is your way of working together for a common purpose. It's also your willingness to be helpful to others. You may be remembering your school days where often you were grouped for something or other. And on a number of occasions you must have been the group / team leader of your group. It's the help and support that you expect from each member of your group for the success of your team. And it's the help and whole hearted support you provide as a member of a group or team for its success is called as co-operation. There, contribution by each member of the group matters.

Self-discipline

It's the control over yourself, your body and mind as well. A control over your likes and dislikes, following a daily routine, the way you plan your personal things and following them very meticulously. At your school and colleges, by following the various instructions, rules and regulations you are creating a self-discipline.

Sportsman spirit

Everyone has an ambition in life to fulfil. It could be to score a very high grading and to top the class, or may be to be the best all around student of your class or school/ college, or to win in a game or tournament, or to possess a high qualification or to get a job of your liking.

It is always good to be optimistic and work towards achieving your aim. At the same time you all know that every one cannot become the winner. Winning and loosing are part of the game. Somebody has to win and somebody has to be the looser and it could be your turn.

One should not feel disappointed in the defeat. Remember, 'Defeat is the key to Success'. It gives you a chance to realize your weaknesses, overcome them and come out successful in your next attempt.

Cheerful

Being cheerful is a God's gift. Having a little smile on your face always dissolves a tense situation. Problems and worries are always part of our life. But they should not affect your professional life. Though this may sound little odd, you can always create such a situation by practicing over the years.

Negative Qualities

Rigid

It's being stiff or being stubborn, not bending or yielding to anything, sticking to your ideas or decisions whether they are right or wrong. It may affect you personally, your friends and others. It is a negative quality and if not controlled, it can even cause damages beyond imagination as you grow up.

Aggressive

It is the tendency to react very strongly or in a forceful way in a situation either among your colleague or with your superiors. You may have a difference of opinion or you may not like the idea or you may have difficulty in accepting a task given to you. But instead of reacting in a normal/ sober/ cool manner, you react in an offensive manner. This will bring in a bad impression about your personal character. It can create an ill feeling or abrasion between the person with whom you reacted and you. And it can even affect your career prospects in that organization.

It's also a negative personal quality and you need to control your feelings/ views and react in a normal way without creating a situation. It also creates unnecessary tension, which will again affect your performance.

Shyness

Getting easily frightened or becoming nervous in the presence of others is quite common in certain people. This definitely you would have felt and experienced in your school or college days. When asked to address the class or perform something, you would have felt shy. In a way it's the lack of self-confidence. You are scared to face others especially a gathering and things become worse when it comes to an unknown crowd. It could be your lack of communication skill, or may be you are an introvert. You always try to keep away from the crowd. This again is a negative personal quality and you need to improve upon by building up your self-confidence, mingling with people, talking to them, taking part in discussions etc.

Observe and Absorb

You all know that you start possessing these personal qualities from your childhood, to begin with, from your own homes and then from your schools and later from others and from your surroundings.

As you grow these personal qualities get absorbed in your life style without you being aware of the fact.

In your day today life and during your interaction with others you see and learn a number of personal qualities. Therefore, you must follow a simple principle of **'Observe and Absorb'.** You may observe many things from your surroundings. But you should absorb only those good qualities, which you think are very much needed to improve your personal and professional life.

Over the years these personal qualities become stronger. Therefore, you need to control them. You must be able to eliminate your bad qualities, absorb and develop good personal qualities and improve them and build a 'personality' that suits you the best.

Leadership Qualities

While all the above qualities will help you to meet with reasonable success in your life, there are certain other qualities, which will take you to the top, to greater achievements. They are called leadership qualities. And they generally include Initiative and Drive, Dependability, Adaptability, Flexibility, Co-operation, Loyalty, Good decision making and Good physical strength. Some of them are valued differently for different career patterns.

A person with these personalities is graded high over a normal person. These are qualities that make a person more matured, more practical, more capable to be able to lead a team, a group or an organization to success, especially in a crisis.

Initiative and Drive

It is the willingness and the driving force behind a person, which make him to take initiative to do a thing and in the same line of thinking as that of his superiors.

In our day to day life you come across a number of situations where you find that people are waiting for some one to take some lead or initiative. There may be more people willing to do a thing but they need someone to take initiative and to lead them.

In areas where you are confronted with high risk jobs you are often tempted not to take any initiative or to avoid the situation by various ways like being absent on the particular moment or day, or showing that you are already involved in some other important work etc. Whereas in such situations, if you are really sincere to yourself and to your profession you will definitely show initiative and drive to do that work. It is also a reflection of your courage and strength.

Dependability

It's a feeling that you create in others that they can depend on you, which again is a vital quality to grade you over others.

It begins at your home. Your approach and actions help your parents and other members of the family to build confidence in you. They get a feeling that they can depend on you on many things. It also helps to build mutual confidence among family members.

Anywhere, whether in your personal life or in your profession, you need to share responsibilities. It is often an organizational requirement for better functioning and better performance. At times you are given independent works, which may form part of a major work program. At times your boss may entrust you with some special assignments to be completed within a specific time frame.

While your timely completion and the quality of your work will be appreciated, any delay or a bad quality of work can cause tremendous pressure on everyone especially when working against time and resources. This kind of situation can adversely affect your career prospects. And on the other hand if you are graded as dependable by your colleagues and seniors and boss it can definitely improve your career prospects.

Adaptability

You must be able to get adjusted to different situations or conditions. During your school days, it's your ability to adapt yourself to new friends, new students in your class, new teachers, new schools and new places if your parents have transferable jobs or when your family moves from one place to another. At times you might find it difficult to adjust. But then gradually you get used to the new atmosphere and may be you like the new place more than other places.

When you get your first job, you need to leave your home and family to a new place, to meet new people, new friends and new working environment. You may not be even satisfied with your job responsibilities. But then you need to get adjusted to these life-changes. It's the only way you can make your own life comfortable. And they are going to repeat themselves in your future career prospects like your transfers from one department to another, transfer from one place to another, change of organization for promotions or new career opportunities etc.

Earlier and easier you are able to adapt yourself to a changing situation the better it is; because it will help you and give you confidence to grow up in any given situation.

Flexibility

Flexibility is the ability of a person to modify or change his plan of action according to given circumstances. It could be within the existing system or in a new situation. In other words, it is the flexibility of mind of an individual to face unforeseen and new challenges.

It is the need for not being so rigid in your decisions and plan of action. There may be some unforeseen and changing or even some challenging situations that may come up. Under such circumstances, one need to modify or work out a plan altogether different if need be and take on the challenges and come out quite successful.

Such a quality will also help you to do well in a crisis management.

Co-operation

As children if you have understood its meaning and realised its need and effect in your school years then you can very well imagine its impact in your future life whether personal or professional.

The demanding needs, the increased cost of living etc. have forced changes in the life style. It has almost become a common sight where both husband and wife take up some job so that they are able to meet the growing demands. It helps them to lead a comfortable life. And both are committed to their family and their profession. It's here your cooperation comes in your family life.

At your work place, it is your co-operation with your colleagues, your fellow workers and other staff of your organization.

Today, with the new work culture, one cannot do things on one's own. And it has necessitated in evolving a system to involve the efforts of everybody in the team, each pulling their weight and contributing in full measure. It has become vital therefore to generate more cooperation and strengthen the bond among the workers.

Your co-operation can create a healthy atmosphere among the members of a group or an organization and give a boost to an existing system. On the other hand, non-cooperation can create a tense atmosphere in an organization and can even affect the mutual relationship and can mark the beginning of disintegration of the system.

Co-operation is very much an essential leadership quality.

Loyalty

Being true and faithful to each other, that's what a husband and a wife look forward to from each other. It makes them live for each other and strengthen their relationship.

It's a similar situation in your professional life. You must be true and faithful in all your activities. It gives you added strength to your inputs. And this reflects in your involvement in the organization you are working.

It's also a feeling and concern that you and your organization are made for each other. You must be loyal to your superiors and to the organization.

Good Decision Making

Decision-making is an art and a good decision making is a 'fine art'. It is the need of the hour today.

In our day to day life you always come across situations where you need to take some decision or other. It may be simple or very difficult decisions. The decisions may be affecting you alone or others including yourself or may be affecting others only.

Another aspect of decision making is the time factor – time available and the time you have taken for making decision. If you have enough time to take a decision then you are able to take a proper decision without any tension. Whereas if you have only a limited time available, then you need to take a quick decision and it may cause tension while taking decision. Further, taking a difficult decision under such circumstances makes it all the more difficult. And credibility of such decisions may be worth a revaluation.

How often you had to change or cancel your decision? It's a big question. It reflects on your ability for taking a good decision.

Ideally, you must be able to take good decisions within the given time frame and right decisions, which do not require any changes or cancellation.

By the way, how do you go about judging a good decision making? Well, check on the following aspects of decision making.

- Are you able to take a suitable decision within the given timeframe?
- Did your decision require any later changes or cancellation?
- What is its effect on the affected people or the organization? In the sense, it should create the least damage to men and material within the possible framework.
- Is your decision the best decision that you could probably think of?

Whenever you are facing a situation where you are required to take a decision, follow this procedure. Analyze what does it involve, work out all possible courses that are available, their effect, the input value in terms of resources and outputs. Then shortlist them if you find them too long. Then make a final decision.

A situation may demand very little or some major effort for analysis before arriving at a good decision. Good knowledge helps to take a good decision. Always try to take a decision, which you need not change or cancel. A good decision is never changed.

Making a timely decision is also equally important. Because, any decision if not taken within the time frame is of no use.

A good decision making often becomes instrumental for your career success.

Good Physical Strength

'A healthy mind in a healthy body. Lucky are those who are able to maintain a healthy body and live long. Good physical health is the prime requisite for your personal success. It's God's blessing that you are born natural. The handicapped should not feel otherwise. Even they can find their way to success provided they have a 'will to succeed'.

As an individual it's your responsibility to maintain your body health. Apart from your family life any profession demands very good health conditions to face the hardship of your professional life.

Some of the professions demands long hours of continuous working of mental and physical hard labor. A career in the Defense services and other paramilitary organizations also demand excellent physical health conditions, which has a direct bearing on your performance.

But if you are not the lucky enough to enjoy good health even then, you should not loose your heart. Because there are a number of professions that can choose from to suit your physical conditions.

Other Humanitarian Considerations

They are a strong family relationship, respect for others, care for the sick and the aged. These are things, which don't need any further explanations. These are a few qualities, which will make you as balanced personality.

****

Personality

The fast growing Science and Information Technology are really making tremendous progress and changes in our life style beyond imagination. Though it has opened up new chapters in career opportunities, the younger generation today find themselves in quite a confused state of mind in grooming themselves to take on the challenges ahead of them and in selecting a suitable career path and pursuing their higher and professional studies. The information and guidance they get from their parents and surroundings are often felt inadequate.

In order to keep up with the fast growing technological advances and to survive in this new world of Information technology, there have been tremendous changes in every field of activity of any commercial organization.

The QR of the employees has gone up considerably. Now days, companies are looking for candidates with some added qualification in addition to their basic qualification. And a better 'Personality' helps you to win over your other competitors.

It's here that you feel the necessity and importance of possessing and developing a good 'Personality'.

What is Personality?

Personality? Oh! It's for ambitious people, for those who want to do well and come up in their life and get some name and fame.

It is the characteristics and qualities of a person seen as a whole. In a way, it is the reflection of total qualities of a person.

Personality is developing a positive attitude in life, confidence building, discovering one's own hidden assets, tackling failure in life, maintaining a healthy body and a sound mind, following a healthy life style, personal grooming and managing relationships.

A proper balancing of the emotional, physical as well as physiological aspects of your life can help you find your place anywhere under the sun.

Once, I was addressing the whole students of a college on a favorite topic, 'Personality Development'.

'You all must have seen an ad in the TV by some manufacturing company for their finest fabrics for clothing, especially for men.' I began.

Most of the students in the audience nodded their head confirming that they were aware of such an ad.

'What does that ad highlight?' I asked.

'About a Complete Man.' they said.

'Yes. It is the notion of a 'Complete man'. What strikes your mind there is not the fabric really, but the lingering memory of an ideal man who is both strong and harbours soft feelings, someone who can be hard and be gentle at the same time. It is basically interplay of contrasts, which any man would love to be, any woman would want in her husband and children in their father. The ad merely projects a certain image of a man with a powerful personality.'

'But that is in the world of imagination, assuming no such men exist. Coming down to the more practical world of people living around us.... Why do we have so much respect for Gandhi? This frail man was responsible for the break up of an empire where 'sun never set'! How did he do it? By his sheer determination. *Success is not defined by the strength but by the indomitable will to succeed.'*

Haven't you heard about those great personalities? Mahatma Gandhi, Abraham Lincoln, Pandit Nehru, John F Kennedy, Winston Churchill, Indira Gandhi and so on.

Generally, when we think about people with great personality, we remember the names of those famous political leaders and statesmen than the names of other great people known for equally better achievements if not more.

And how do we grade their personality? Great, High, Good, Strong, Negative, Pleasing, Beautiful and so on?

What is the correct way of grading a personality? Can we say, 'He has a high personality'? Or can we say, 'He has a good personality'? Or can we say, 'She has a beautiful personality'?

At times we are ignorant of what we say. Because we don't mean what we say and we don't say what we really mean.

Mostly it is the wrong notion about the word 'Personality' that people are confused. They often fail to understand its real meaning and its effect on their personal lives.

Personality has a great bearing on your lives, your career, the organization you are working, society around you and your own country as a whole.

Personal qualities of a grown up or a matured person shall include among others, appearance and bearing, self-confidence, determination, hardworking, sincere, willing, honest, punctuality, responsible, trustworthiness and self-discipline.

Let us consider each one of them to see how they affect your overall personality.

Appearance and Bearing

It is the impression a person creates in his mind when looking at you. As the good old saying goes, 'First impression is the best impression' it matters. It includes your physical figure, your dress and your hairstyle. Your eyes and your expressions also matter because they also add to the impression you create in another person looking at you.

It speaks of your need to be neat and tidy, wearing a dress appropriate to the occasion, with a hairstyle that suits you the best and an expressive look in your eyes.

Wearing a dress appropriate to the occasion is very important be it an interview or at your profession. If you are presenting yourself at an interview, you need to wear a dress that suits you and the profession for which you are being interviewed for. Like for example, a teacher should be wearing a modest dress in the class room, a model need to wear a costume that is expected to bring in an impact on the viewers, a business executive will have to wear a dress to impress upon the customers and so on.

These are only guidelines and it's all up to your judgment to give the correct impression about you to the other person, it could be your friend, your lover, your students, your audience, your boss, the customers or your interviewer.

Most of the companies expect their employees to look smart. Companies manufacturing pharmaceutical products and dealing in health care products insist their employees to be personally more hygiene to ensure quality products. It is also very much needed for those who have to work very close to each other or interact with others.

Self-confidence

It is a commonly understood personal quality, especially so because of the media publicity for a number of consumer products like tooth paste, deodorant, toilet soaps, mouth wash etc. use of which generates a self-confidence in you as the advertisers claim.

Is it the same type of self-confidence that we are referring in this contest? In a way such self-confidence gives you confidence to present yourself while approaching others or interacting with others where you need to work closely.

But is that the kind of self-confidence you are looking for? No, definitely not. It is the confidence you have about yourself after fully knowing well about your abilities, in other words your worth and potential. It is also a feeling that 'I can do it'.

For this, you need to explore yourself and identify your potential whether tried or untried out abilities. Open up yourself, try out things which you want to make a beginning. Thus, gradually you will be able to identify your abilities.

This is the greatest blessing one could have, *having a tremendous self-confidence*. And it has greater contribution to your personality. Like many other qualities this is also developed over the years as you grow.

Success is not defined by strength but the indomitable will to succeed.

Some years ago, I remember watching one of those beauty contests – I forget if it was Miss World or Miss Universe. In the second round of the competition where the judges ask questions to the short-listed ten contestants, one judge asked a contestant: 'If you were to describe yourself in two words, what will they be?'

A simple question with a difficult answer! You need to describe everything that you want to convey about yourself, in just two words.

The answer still rings in my ears. She looked straight into the judge's eyes and said, 'Self-confident and determined'.

Beautiful, I thought. One couldn't have better expressed than that. It contained everything that she wanted to convey about her.

This is a very good live example for self-confidence.

Determination

It is a 'Will to Do', rather a 'Will to Do to Succeed'. And this is another strong personal quality, which also has a great bearing on your personality. It's also a feeling that 'I will do it'.

You all know, things don't work out that simple as we think, especially now a days. You need to work for it. Not only you need to have a 'Will to Do' but also a 'Will to Succeed' in what you are doing. Only then you can taste success.

Determination is the power you generate within yourself to work hard and try hard and keep trying until you succeed. A strong personality comes from a strong WILL.

It's a story of a college student. She was studying for her final year B.A. in a women's college and she wanted to become the chairperson of her college.

Being the daughter of a parent with a transferable job she had widely travelled all over India. This gave her more exposure and had very good command and fluency in English language.

She along with her friends did a good campaign work and was confident of her winning. The result came and to her surprise she lost in the election. The only reason for her defeat was her inability to communicate well in the regional language Malayalam to the students, which they expected from their chairperson to be more effective.

Obviously she was upset over this. But she never expressed her feelings outside. Her parents and friends consoled her. Next year she joined for PG classes in the same college. She let the first year go. And she was in her final year M.A.

One evening she told her parents, 'Daddy, there is a surprising news for you. Once again I'm contesting for the post of Chairperson of our college this year. I promise, it will not affect my studies in anyway.' She added.

She wanted to make up the only weak point she had of her loosing battle and wanted to put in her best during this year. She had tremendous self-confidence and a strong will power to do and to succeed.

It was a day where the contesting candidates presented themselves in front of the whole college students in the college auditorium and gave a brief talk about their manifesto and plan of action if elected to the post of chairperson.

When her turn came, she came to the dais, looked at the crowd for a moment. More than half the students of the college had seen her giving a similar speech earlier where she had lost to her opponent. Everyone became silent and anxiously waited to listen to her words.

She began her speech in pure Malayalam language, no mix up what so ever. Her speech was so impressive and inspiring that there was frequent cheering from the crowd. It was the best speech they had heard that day. Everyone looked to be very happy about her performance.

And that year she was elected as their college chairperson with a record margin. It was quite an impressive victory for the whole college, and an important landmark in her life. *It was a victory of her self-confidence and unbeatable determination.*

And do you know the secret of her success?

Having fully aware of her weak point 'not been able to talk to the students in Malayalam' during her loosing election campaign earlier, this time she was determined to give a talk to the students in Malayalam, their regional language. And she was prepared to do everything for it.

One of her closest friends helped her in this venture. Her friend wrote down a beautiful inspiring speech in Malayalam on the guidelines that she had told her to write. Once the speech was edited, she wrote down the same Malayalam speech in Hindi, in which she was also very good, so that she could pronounce the Malayalam words correctly and easily. She then prepared her speech very well and presented herself on that day. Nobody else except her closest friend knew about this secret. She is one of the most remembered students and chairpersons of her college even today.

This is a clear example of 'tremendous self-confidence, sheer determination and a strong will power'.

Hardworking

Handwork is the key word to success. Remember there are no shortcuts to success. You need to physically and mentally work to achieve success.

Whether it's in your personal life or professional life hard work will always provide you with some positive end results. At times though you may find it difficult in your initial attempt, your hard work will lead your way through to your success.

The earlier example of the college student is also an excellent example of hard work. It was her hard work coupled with her tremendous self-confidence and sheer determination that made her glorious victory possible.

You must be very familiar with the working style of people. Some are very casual. Some are very fast and some work at a reasonable speed. What really needed is to work with care and at a reasonable speed without wasting time and effort. And that is what you must develop.

Sincere

It's yet another good personal quality, being sincere to self and to others. It's a genuine effort you reflect in your words and actions, whether it is for yourself or dealing with others. It may be an offer for help you are making to others, it may be a piece of advice and guidance you are giving to somebody, it may be your own work at your office.

Willing

It is the *Will to learn* and the *Will to do* and is a positive sign of progress. Whether it is in your home or at your work place you must have a *will to work*. Willingness should come from within you. Never try to do a thing as if it has been forced upon you. Only then you will feel happy and contented in your work.

During the course of your career there can be a number of occasions where you may come across work that you may not like to do. But you need to accept them as part of your duty. Some of such jobs though initially you may find difficult, later as you start doing you will start liking them. If you are working in an organization, your active participation is also required for the successful growth of your organization. Even, you must be willing to accept additional responsibilities if required in case of any crisis.

Integrity

It is a quality of being honest and morally upright, a quality that always you do only the 'right' things and stand by the truth.

When we talk about integrity we are reminded of a small incident from Gandhi's early life. You all know about that story. When he was studying in the school, the school inspector made a surprise visit to their school and took a dictation test. Gandhi did not know how to spell *kettle*. Even when his teacher instigated him to cheat, Gandhi was adamant; he said that he didn't know the answer and will NOT cheat! That's integrity.

Integrity cannot be rated in terms of percentage, like 90% or 95%. Either you have it or don't have it. And this basic and important quality you learn along with other personal qualities from your childhood, at home, at school and as you grow up in your life.

It has a greater dimension when dealing with financial matters. It reflects the delicate side of personality of a person. It is something that people look for in a person when being considered to hold very critical and high office, especially when it involves very sensitive issues and temptations.

One may prove to be very honest in petty things but may be tempted to be dishonest when it involves financial matters and monetary gains. It is a quality that makes you to deal with any issues, big or small, whether it involves monetary gain or not, in an impartial way, owning up on your own mistakes or lapses, giving a fair judgement and being honest to yourself and being morally upright.

Whereas all other personal qualities have direct effect on an individual, this personal quality has an effect on others life too. And therefore, integrity is graded very high over the other personal qualities. A person with integrity is always looked upon very high everywhere whether it is an organization, society or country.

It helps you to build confidence in others and also helps you to build mutual relationship with others.

Integrity is another factor, which will push you up in the ladder in your pursuit for brighter career prospects.

Punctuality

It's very simple for all to understand though it might look difficult to practice in their real life. May be it's because they don't understand the 'real importance' of this personal quality. It's something we expect from others or rather expect others to follow. But when it comes to your own action, you often find excuses for being late.

In a world with such a fast advancement of science and technology, we must realise the value of time. It's priceless. Every second matters. We must realise its value as important to you is to others or may be even more valuable to others.

Specially so for the personal interviews, companies often allot block timings to the candidates so that no body waists time in too much waiting and the candidates are expected to report for interviews at the given date and time. And you know well, if you don't report in time, you often have a high risk of missing or loosing that interview.

Even during your career, there will be ample opportunities for you to meet other people of your own or of other companies or organizations for official matters. It could be a personal meeting, could be a group meeting, it could be a business meeting. And there is no need to emphasis the need for one to be very punctual on such occasions. Being not punctual can also cause tremendous damage and loss of business activities and can directly affect your career.

Responsible

It is your commitment that you are answerable for your behavior and actions.

During the course of your personal and professional life you undertake and carry out a number of tasks given to you or may be accepted by your initiative and you try to do or complete them to the best of your ability. Because you know the things you do may affect adversely your personal life or may affect a continuous system of the organization you are working.

You must have a sense of responsibility for whatever you do and you should also have the moral courage to accept the consequence that may arise out of your action.

This will help others in grading you as a person who can be relied upon or as a person who can be depended upon. And depending on your ability to accept and shoulder responsibility, you will be entrusted with higher responsibilities, which prove your professional ability.

This personal quality has a bearing in judging your personality.

Trustworthy

It's a quality where others grade your credibility to trust whether they can trust you with anything that they want to confide in you. It can be in your personal life, like between a husband and wife, between parents and their children, between other family members and your friends.

And in your professional career it can be between your fellow workers, with your subordinates and also with your superiors. It's the mutual trust you build up among your colleagues, with your subordinates and your superiors. You need to develop a mutual trust among others especially your colleagues and others of the organisation you are working. It will definitely help you in your career prospects.

Self-discipline

It is the control over yourself, following a routine that is best suited to your personal as well as professional life.

In a way, it is a grouping of a few personal qualities like, punctuality, sense of responsibility, sincerity. It has a direct bearing on your personality.

Effect of punctuality is known to all of us as we have well experienced in our lives. We always appreciate a person who is very punctual and doesn't keep others waiting. It teaches the value for time to you and to others. It becomes more important when giving an appointment to anyone or taking an appointment from anyone and adhering to the given commitment.

Sense of responsibility is also a part of your self-discipline. You must feel responsible for the things you are doing. You also need to own up the responsibility for the work/ action you have done whether they are right or wrong.

Whether at home or at your place of work it helps you to set everything in order following a better working system. This will help you to get maximum output with minimum resources.

You will realise that by creating self-discipline you can avoid almost half the confusion in your life, whether it is your personal life or professional life.

A good self-discipline also gets you an appreciation from others.

The Icing
So now the cake is all made. But you know, icing adds the attraction. And that's where you add the following.
Be cheerful,
Develop a good communication and interpersonal skill, and add a sense of humor

Be Cheerful
Being cheerful is a God's gift. We always love to see a cheerful face. Having a little smile on your face always dissolves a tense situation. Problems and worries are always part of our life. Some of the things if covered behind a cheerful face you can even avoid a lot of tension among your own family members. Your problems and worries in no way should affect your professional life.

Though this may sound little odd, you can always create such a situation by practicing over the years.

Good Communication and Interpersonal Skill
'A good communication skill and interpersonal skill' are the key words to success today.

In this ever-growing world of competition, the demand for excellence in every field is increasing day by day. And it calls for perfection in every field of activity. Further, in the wake of globalization, interaction between the countries on the international business and political relationship has increased.

The need for a good interpersonal skill within the organization and corporate levels and with outside agencies has become a must for a better output in the present scenario. Further, a good interpersonal skill and a good communication skill at the middle, senior and top management levels are the call of the day.

More emphasis is being given to improve the quality of the existing management staff at various levels and care is taken to recruit highly qualified managerial staff with a better interpersonal skill and good communication skill. This clearly speaks of the requirement of the day.

Often lack of communication or bad communication can cause a lot of misunderstanding and may lead into unwarranted situations.

It's imperative for you to improve your own spoken language and practice it with your friends to improve your communication skill. Use of a courteous language will always pay dividend.

Thus, an individual with good interpersonal skill and a good communication skill along with other qualifications has a better chance of success over others.

Add a Sense of Humor

In our day to day life we have often seen some people even with their normal conversation make us laugh. At times they give us some break from our tense moments. It is a gift to be humorous and make others laugh. It is an ability to use apt words at the right place and time and to the right person.

It is also important to possess a sense of humor. Or else you may not be able to appreciate a humor. At times some people try to be humorous to dilute a serious or a tense situation. So others must be able to understand the situation and try to appreciate the humor and not make the scene more tense.

A sense of humor during your short break or free time can make a difficult and tense situation in your office into a comfortable, relaxed and enjoyable atmosphere, especially so in the present new world of science and information technology where the new 'work culture' has proved to be most effective and result oriented.

****

Grooming

It's quite possible that over the years, most of you have someone in your mind as your role model, that you adore or rather you have very high impression due to his or her charisma.

Whenever you look at or hear about some great people like Gandhi, Pundit Nehru, Indira Gandhi, Winston Churchill etc. You often make a wish, 'if you could become some one like them'.

But if somebody ask me such a question, I would say 'No. I don't want to become like someone. I want to develop a personality of my own.' And it is true.

The same thing I would advise you too. Why should you try to copy someone or try to become like someone?

Do you know? Every one of you is the 'blessed creations' of God the Almighty. And every one of you is blessed with immense number of personal qualities. You must go deep inside and identify those invaluable qualities and abilities.

Develop on those qualities and improve upon them. All you know, you may become a greater personality than what you thought to be. Wouldn't it be a great achievement? Yes, indeed.

When and where do you begin?

*You learn them in **three** stages.*

- You begin to learn them *at your home*, from your parents and from other members of your family,
- You learn them *at your school* from other students of your school and from teachers and also from the surroundings, and
- You also learn them from others and *on your own*.

Each stage of learning is very important. Because you learn them at different levels and your level of understanding is different at those levels. It's a continuous process of learning.

As you grow, after your studies you take up a job. It gives you totally a different experience altogether. Perhaps the first time you start interacting with the outside world, a professional world where everything is viewed in a more professional manner. All of a sudden you find a lot more to learn, a lot of self-adjustments to be made to be able to be part of the team or a group or an organization.

The Right Time

The learning power in children is much more than in adults and the learning process is also faster as compared to that is in the adults.

In the present arrangement of school and college studies, students are able to complete their education up to Plus Two (12th Grade) in their school itself. And only higher / professional education is continued at the college / university level.

The physical transformation of the children takes place mostly during the period of their school education i.e. by the time they finish their Plus Two (12th grade) education.

With the advancement of science and technology you must realize that you are living in a fast changing world. Everything about your life style is changing so fast that you need to work hard to cope up with the changes. These changes have also materially affected the family life. Children learn a lot more from the surroundings than they used to learn earlier and also at a faster pace.

This cautions how careful the parents should be in taking care of their growing children. It's something like one becoming more careful and cautious while driving fast. The lifestyle and systems are changing so fast that if proper care and guidance are not given to the children, they are likely to get into the wrong direction. Therefore, it would be better to care and guide the children at the appropriate time as they grow than trying to bring back a spoiled child into the right track.

A close monitoring in the development of children and a proper guidance will always help them come up to your expectations.

The Widening Gap

The biggest problem most of the parents face today is the changing personal relationship between them and their children. They feel there is a gap between them and their grown up children and they are worried that this gap is widening day by day.

Why should there be a gap at all between the parents and their children? Is it because they don't understand each other's language? Or is it that either of them does not make enough efforts to understand each other and care for each other? And why should such a situation come up in your family life? What are the reasons attributing to this phenomenon? How can we overcome such situation?

This is the situation most of the parents face in their families today. This situation can be easily improved 'provided they have a *Will* to do so and sincerely work towards it'.

But how? It's very simple. You know children in their tender age learn everything very fast. Therefore, you, the parents should take care of your children from their very early stage itself.

Role of Parents

Children as they grow learn from their parents and other members in their family. They also learn a lot from what they see and hear in the family. Children have very good grasping/ assimilation power and therefore they pick up things very fast.

This makes it all the more important for the parents to create a good family environment at their homes, and guide and teach their growing children about various personal qualities.

A loving and stimulating environment at home is a must for the child's self-development.

Even if you have to make some sacrifices in your words, actions and your life style, you have to do it for the sake of your children.

We know about the life style we follow in most of the families. In good old days, only father used to go for work outside and usually mother stayed at home taking care of the household affairs. So mother always got more time with the children. Further, in a large/ joint family, there were others also to take care of the children. The roles of grandpas and grandmas were great. Mostly it was through them that the children in such families learned about various personal qualities.

Today, the demanding needs, the increased cost of living etc. have forced changes in the life style. It has almost become a common sight where both husband and wife take up some job so that they are able to meet the growing demands. It helps them to lead a comfortable life. Most of the parents want to give everything that they had missed or get in their younger days and go all out to provide everything to their children. Most of the day they are out for their job and they hardly get any time to look after their children and for giving the required individual care and attention to them.

In certain cases though the parents may be willing they often fail in their duties as parents. The work pressure and tension at their work places often add fuel to the already squeezed life style. The family life becomes more of a 'mechanical life'. Every second is accounted for and everything works like the needles of an hour clock.

Thus most of the parents anxiously wait for their children to become about three years old so that they can send them to a nursery school. And then rest every thing they leave it to the teachers and to the school authorities as responsible for their good academic progress and development of their personal qualities.

Your efforts don't stop the day you start sending your children to the school. While the learning process and overall development continues at the school, your guidance and care of your children should continue as they grow.

It's much more important to provide a good family atmosphere than you provide all other things for their physical comforts. It is not that you provide every thing to your children and you expect your children to grow up as good children with all ideal personal qualities. No, they need a constant guidance and help especially so in this fast growing world.

As parents you must love your children, understand their potential, their desire, ambitions in life and their weakness. Only then you will be able to guide and help them.

Whether big or small you must appreciate their achievements and try to encourage them in their efforts. This will boost their self-confidence.

You need to build up confidence in each other. And as parents you should take initiative in this process.

They must get convinced that you are very much interested in their growth and future as they do. Only then they will listen to you and take your words.

Look at the progress made in the field of science and technology and the changes that brought into our life style. In order to move along with this technological progress, you need to take more interest in such developments.

It has also brought in changes in the career pattern and career prospects. Therefore you need to gain some minimum knowledge so that you are able to give some minimum guidance about the future prospects to your children.

We all know that all parents have very high expectations from their children, to study well, score a high grading, continue higher education and finally get a very good job, which should give him enough financial security to be able to lead a comfortable life.

But you often fail to guide and help and give necessary inspiration and motivation to our children to come up in line of your expectations. This is where you need to concentrate and pay more attention.

Never blame or curse them for little things. Inspire them with good stories and life incidents. Teach them about the moral values of life. Give courage and strength to them in their weak moments. Spend some time together with your children. Try to have some meals together. Plan some outings, within your budget, with your family members. This will improve the personal relationship a lot.

An important point the parents should understand is that they should broaden their views and interact with their growing children in a friendlier manner.

A home is a platform on which the children are able to build their future plans and work towards them. It's a 'Launching Pad' from where children can take off to their world of growth and prosperity. It's a platform from where the children can look forward to re-launch their new plans if the first one fails or does not meet with success as they had expected. It's a platform for their overall development.

Whatever small things parents do for their children, strengthen their self-confidence and hope for building up a bright career for their future. *Your appreciation even over their small achievements, your guidance, consent, support and encouragement are always the strongholds of their success and provides the thrust for their take off to their own future world.*

Thus it is very important to give emphasis on the character formation in early part of children's life and give due care and attention on their personality development as they grow. Only then you can expect your children to grow up as good children and live up to your expectations. Only by this you will be able to groom your children, the future generation for a better tomorrow.

Role of Teachers

While the 'base' or 'foundation' of a child's growth and future is built at their homes, further growth of knowledge and personal qualities are built during their school and college/ higher studies. Here they come to a common place where they meet children from different family set up, different family background and children with different culture.

And it's here the role of Teachers come into play. Everything they can do, from developing a child into an ideal student to leaving them to their own plight thus ruining them, their life and future. Everything depends on the personal qualities of the teacher and the teacher-student relationship.

It is the tender age from eight to say about thirteen or fourteen years of a child, which is the critical period of a child. It's a period during which the learning ability is at the peak of their life. It's a period where we can moderate on their personal qualities and help them to mould their character, physical and mental growth. But this can be achieved only through the dedicated effort of a teacher.

I still remember, at one 'peace station' during my service in the army my wife, though a double graduate was teaching at one of those Army Children School where children from nursery to UKG were taught. She often used to discuss with me her school activities of the children in her class and the way those little children behaved and how she handled them.

Whether it was English or any other subject, she gave individual care to each student. Accordingly she used to plan her teaching. Sometimes I really used to wonder at the interest and effort she took to teach those tiny tots. But she was very happy and found pleasure in her work. Often it was a sight to see the parents expressing their gratitude to her for the improvement their children had shown both at their homes and in their knowledge. Their children accepted everything the teacher taught them as 'Gospel Truth'. Because, even at their age, they knew that teacher will only teach them the truth and nothing but truth.

It is this feeling the children carry about their teachers and it has a great impact over their life. And that's how we say that a teacher plays a major role in the growth and development of a child by teaching them about various personal qualities, guiding and helping them to develop those personal qualities to their best advantage and above all inspiring them to put in their best in their studies. In fact they can do wonders.

This can only be achieved if the teachers are sincere and dedicated to their profession.

They need to accept as if the students are their own children. Try to identify every student by name, understand about their family background, learn about their weak and strong points, and explore their hidden strength and talents. Win their confidence that you are doing every thing for their own good.

Appreciation and motivation are two very important factors in bringing up the children.

Teachers should be more concerned about their overall developments and performance than on their mere academic grading.

The teachers should take initiative and use innovative ideas and methods in their teaching plan highlighting the values of human life. After all, today's children are tomorrow's youth. They spend their prime period of growth at schools and colleges.

Teachers are the best architects for transforming the children into ideal citizens of tomorrow.

Only they can create the better citizens of tomorrow. Thus teachers play a vital role in grooming the future citizens of our country and in a way they are responsible for the quality of the citizens of our country.

Does your Name affect your Personality?

Well, there is a mixed reaction to this whether it may or may not affect your personality. It's a matter of individual opinion.

Parents are always anxious about their newborn baby and about the name they want to give to their newborn. Whereas in some parts of the country people follow some traditional customs for naming their new born, most of the parents look for a name that is very unique, especially so in the present fast changing world scenario.

While some parents feel that by giving a particular name, their child will grow up and keep up the meaning and status of that name. Others name their children by the name of a person / personality they admire in their life.

Once we had invited applications for the posts of Sales Executives for our company. While scanning through the applications of the short listed candidates for the personal interview, I noticed the name of a candidate as 'Napoleon'. I was little amused. It made me anxious to know the background that made his parents give that name to their newborn. And I looked forward to meet him at the personal interview.

At the personal interview I met Mr. Napoleon. He was an average built person. During the initial phase of the interview I asked him, which I had been anxiously waiting for, 'What was the secret behind your getting the name Napoleon?'

He smiled at me and said, 'Sir, this a question often lots of people have asked me.' He continued, 'My father was an ardent admirer of Napoleon. And the only way to express his admiration towards Napoleon was to name me after his name, he says. And thus I became Napoleon, an emperor without an empire.' He still had his smile on his face.

Look at the craze of the parents!

Years later, one day after I had finished my talk on 'Personality Development' at a college, a few students came to me to convey their personal appreciation and also to clarify some of their anxious points. During my interaction with them one girl introduced herself as 'Flower' with a smile.

'What? I wanted to confirm whether I heard her correctly.

And she knew why I asked her that question. She said again, 'Flower.'

I couldn't believe that she could have such a name.

I asked her, 'How do you spell it?' I wanted to know if it was the same 'Flower' or some other 'Folver'.

Again, with a smile she said, 'F L O W E R'. She spelt it very clearly.

At this, other students standing nearby had a big smile.

When I knew that her name had the same spelling as for 'Flower' I was really astonished. Here again, look at the craze of the parents and the family members!

You also must have come across, some names like, Dolly, Pussy, Sweety, Lousy, Unni (means a small child in Malayalam) etc. These names may look to be all right for young children. But when they grow up into a matured person, often these names cause quite an embarrassment to them.

Once I happened to see an interesting programme, in one of the TV channels. It was an inter-active programme with people having very attractive and notable names on one side and some audience on the other side.

The anchor of the TV show in his introduction said that he was delighted to introduce a few people with some attractive and notable name, which often caused embarrassment to others to call them by their name. The audience also included some of the parents who had named their children with their innovative idea. And the show began.

Two of the individuals (adult) names were 'Castless Senior' and Castless Junior'. The anchor then asked their parents as to what motivated them in naming their children with such names.

Their father promptly said. 'You see, ours was a love marriage. I am a Muslim and the girl whom I loved was a Christian and therefore, there was lot of opposition to our marriage. So in order to express our protest against people's attitude towards inter cast marriage, we decided to name our son as 'Castless' meaning a person with no particular cast or religion. But when we had our second son, we gave them names as 'Castless Senior' and 'Castless Junior'.'

To a question to the individuals (Castless Senior and Castless Junior) as to what were their reaction when they grew up and what they felt when others called them by their names, they said that they didn't find anything wrong with their parents in naming them with such names.

But when the audience asked them as to from which cast or religion would they marry and what names they would give to their children, their replies and reactions were quite embarrassing.

In another case, a father had named his three sons as Neutron, Proton, and Electron'.

Is your father a scientist? The TV anchor asked with a smile. Well, it wasn't so.

Then he must be 'Nucleus'?

'No', was their answer.

Even the audiences were quite confused.

Their father, ex-defence employee had his version. He believed in 'no cast and creed' and he also knew that *unity* is required for the existence of the world.

Yet in another case a father by name *'Earnest'* had named his son as *'Wisemon'* and his daughter as *'Nicemol'*.

It was quite interesting to note the parent's reasoning in naming their children with such 'wonderful names' and the reaction from the audience.

Often one tends to forget the impact in naming his children with such names, especially when his children grow up in the society. It is a 'life long' identity that we are giving to our children. Therefore, the names should be such that they suit the children when they grow up as per your expectations and should not cause any embarrassments to them. In certain cases some children change their names by following a formal procedure. But then, why to wait for such a situation

It's for the parents to be more sensible and careful in naming their children.

How to Develop your Personality?

Very often, people anxiously look at 'Personality Development' as something like a *'Quick Action Program'*, which you can undergo and see the results instantly. It's only the lack of awareness about 'Personality Development' that one tends to think in such a way.

In its literal sense, it's a 'Self-improvement', like improving your health and your overall development. Depending on your personal qualities, you may require less or more effort to improve your personal qualities and for your personality development.

And it's you who need to put in the physical effort of improving yourself. And therefore, it all depends on your 'WILL' to improve and your 'WILL' to work.

If you possess these, then it's very SIMPLE. Try. Make a beginning.

You know that you have already made a beginning at your own home. Lucky are those who got a good beginning at their homes? You may be the lucky one to learn about them from your parents and other members of your family. Or may be you are unlucky to learn about them the way you should have learnt due to various avoidable and unavoidable circumstances.

Again, you may be lucky to study in a good school where everything was very ideal and you could learn more about various personal qualities and other leadership qualities. You may have got proper guidance and help at the right time so that you could realise your weaknesses and control your personal qualities to transform yourself into an acceptable personality. Or may be you were the unlucky.

Even after your studies, you would not have got an ideal environment or opportunity to develop yourself into a desired personality. And you may be thirsting to improve your personal qualities and develop your personality as needed and demanded for the success in your life.

So what if you are one of those unlucky people who didn't get the desired opportunities to improve your personality. That should not in any way disappoint you because you haven't lost much in your life. As long as you have realized that you need to develop and improve your personality you are already at a winning start.

There is no specific time or period for a learning process. Of course, there is an ideal time for everything. But if you have missed it due to any reasons, it may or may not be due to your own fault, you can still make it. Your age and position are no restrictions. Provided you have 'A Will to Learn and A will to Work'. That will make everything very simple.

It's your Desire and Will to improve your personality that is most important.

Wherever you are, make a beginning NOW.

- Look at yourself - your dress, your things, your table and the way things are lying around in your room. Do you think you can improve upon them? If so, do that right now. Thinking of doing them later? No. Never. Never postpone anything for tomorrow. Start doing right then and there. It might take some of your time and physical effort. But it is never a waste. It's an effort towards your success.

- Think about various *personal qualities one should have.* And think of the *personal qualities YOU have.* Identify your strong as well as your weak points.
- Identify those personal qualities, which you need to develop and those, which you need to further improve and make a physical effort to develop/ improve them.
- You may be worrying as to how to go about it. It may look difficult but they are never impossible, provided you make a concerted effort. Tackle them one by one.

For example you want to develop or improve a personal quality say 'Punctuality'. It includes, being punctual about timings, sticking to your promises and commitments to others. Start adhering to them by physically doing them. Say, report at the appointed time. If you have to travel for some distance to your office and if there is a possibility of traffic jam, break down of your vehicle including a minor defect or a tyre puncture, you need to plan for some extra time to cater for all these. And not that you find such events as reasons for your being late at the given time. One odd unforeseen incident may be accepted but do not make it a regular habit. Nobody, including you, will ever accept such a person. So why not be punctual.

Another reason could be that you have forgotten about a given appointment or your casual attitude towards such an event, like 'so what if I am late or if I don't make it.' You should never treat them very casually. It can cause great damages to you and to others. The best way to overcome this difficulty is to make a note of such appointments or events in your diary or engagement pads and plan them well ahead.

Similarly, about making promises or giving a commitment to someone, you must stick to them. And if you find that in spite of your earnest efforts you are unable to honor your commitments, it could be due to your bad planning or wrong assessment about your ability or your poor judgement about others.

The best way to overcome this difficulty is to make a correct assessment of the situation whether it is about your own ability or other's. Add little extra time to it to cater for any eventualities. Only then you must give any commitment to others. And once given any commitment, at all cost you must stick to it.

- *Set a realistic ambition in your life and work towards achieving the same.* There is no specific yardstick in terms of size, value and effort for setting your ambition. It will all depend on your desire, age, maturity, qualification, self-confidence, determination and your personality.
- *Self-confidence is an important tool in personality development* and how to develop or improve the same. It's a feeling that you will be able to do the things as you planned and do successfully. Develop that kind of feeling in you.

Self-confidence is something you need to generate within yourself. This calls for a systematic and meticulous planning and execution, taking care of every aspect so that you don't end up in a crisis.

Set achievable targets and try to complete them. This will give you tremendous self-confidence.

As you grow in your life, you must set small things as part of your main ambition. Instead of setting a single ambition like 'to get a good job and to live a happy family life', you must set intermediate aims, like a good education with a high grading, a good career, a personal conveyance, a good marriage alliance, growth in your profession and a happy family life with your spouse and children, the growth and a bright future for your children and so on.

And you must work hard to achieve you immediate aim and the next and the next and so on. Thus, as you progress in your life, such achievements will boost your self-confidence and self-courage.

Added to improve your personality is 'Determination'. It's your *STRONG WILL POWER to do a thing till you achieve success.* For this *you must have a 'Will to Learn, a Will to Work and Work Hard'.* Some of the things you plan may look difficult or impossible, but with your strong *will power* will make them possible. You may not be successful in your first attempt. But definitely you will meet with success.

'If others can, why can't I?' This question will always prompt you into action.

Tremendous 'self-confidence' with good 'determination' is an excellent combination of personal qualities for your better personality.

You should not expect a win every time. At the same time, you should not get disappointed in your defeat. You should consider your defeat as a key to success and work hard in your next attempt only to find success.

Life is full of events and problems. And there are always solutions to any problems. So, you shouldn't get worried about them. Whenever you face any crisis or problem what you need to do is to analyze thoroughly their good and bad points and then hope for the best but at the same time be prepared for the worst. If you adopt this principle in your life, then you will never have an occasion to repent or have any disappointment in your life.

- *Be always optimistic but never be over optimistic.* If you are over optimistic, it will only bring in disappointment.
- Follow the basic principle of *'A healthy mind in a healthy body'.*

- Build up confidence in others. This you can generate by your inter relation with others, your words and actions.
- *Develop a good communication skill.* A good communication skill and interpersonal skill are other parameters in judging one's personality. It is also required for you to express yourself to others. Often lack of communication or bad communication can cause a lot of misunderstanding and may lead into unwarranted situations.

  You can use simple language to convey your points. Lack of fluency in a language mostly acts as a barrier to a good communication. Therefore, it's imperative for you to improve your own spoken language and practice it with your friends to improve your communication skill. Use of a courteous language will always pay dividend.
- *Being cheerful* can also help you a lot in a situation, which otherwise would have developed into tense moments. It helps you to control your tense moments and can help you to overcome difficult situation when dealing with others. It adds to personality and will give a good impression about you at an interview or at a crucial meeting with others. It's a sign of beginning or revival of a friendship.
- Respect others considering their age, positions and rank, in your words and actions. Avoid discussions and references, which may create an ill feeling among others.
- *Never mix up your profession with your personal life.* That can only cause you problems.
- Always accept and appreciate others ability and their achievements.
- Observe others and absorb only their good things.
- Remember that 'You are your own Master' and everything is under your control. You are the one to decide about your future and nobody else.

Life is a game. Play it well for your own good.

Personal Counseling

It's quite possible that sometimes you get into a situation where things don't work out according to your plan or as expected.

This may bring in you a feeling of rejection because you are not selected or you are not being considered and may cause disappointment or even it might lead you into a state of depression.

Such a situation only reminds you of certain things like, about your ambition, your planning and approach, your effort and your sincerity. Because your over ambition, poor planning, incorrect approach, insufficient effort, all can cause to produce a negative result or a result that is less than your expectation. Under such circumstances you need to review all these aspects and move forward with a new vigor.

When you are in a confused state of mind or in a depression due to something, which you think you can not overcome on your own, it's an indication that you must go for a 'Personal Counseling'. This will help you to identify the problem areas and to overcome such a situation. It will help you to regain your lost hope and self-confidence to win over the hurdles in your life.

A 'Personal Counseling' will also help you to identify any of your unknown potential and it can even give a boost to your self-confidence. And you may be able to set a higher ambition in your life.

Above all, it's your good behavior at home, relationship with your parents and other members of your family to begin with and then your personality that keeps you going in your life.

****

Career

Career is a profession, which will provide opportunities in your life for advancement and promotion. Everyone, after his studies/ higher education/ professional qualification, looks forward to getting a job, a job of his choice or preference, your Dream Profession.

You may have set an ambition in your life. You may have planned your education and may possess qualification to suit your chosen career. But when you apply for a job you find that there are many more like you who have applied for the same job. Though you had full hope of getting into that job, sometime you turned out to be unlucky and somebody else take away that job. Thus, perhaps you have to get contented with some job that come in your way or in a way you are lucky to be selected.

Beggars can't be Choosers. So in most of the cases, you accept the first job that comes in your way. Thus often you may have to get satisfied with a job, which may not be of your choice or preference.

While you may be recruited on the basis of your 'technical and professional skills', your career prospects, say your promotion, perks and other privileges will be based on your 'human relations skills'. *And a number of personal qualities like flexibility, adaptability, co-operation, teamwork etc. are becoming a 'must have qualities' for a successful career life.*

Does Personality affect your Career and your Organization?

Yes, very much. Your personality has an effect on your career and the organization you are working.

During your day to day life, you must have visited a number of offices / organizations for something or other. On such occasions, as you entered the office, the surroundings and your interaction with the staff there would have created some impression about the person you met there, that office or organization in your mind.

The impression could be good or bad. But the fact remains that it's the comparison of reality with your expectations from such an encounter. The overall set up, the communication and the inter-personal skill of the persons you met, the discipline, courtesy, efficiency and so on.

Whether good or bad, it's the words, action and the reflection of the personal qualities of the personnel working there that gave you the impression you carried after visiting that office or organization.

It's the personal qualities that you had developed over the years as you grew, a personality you loved to possess.

How does it affect your Career?

You know well that an 'introvert' is not a good choice for post of a Public Relation Officer, Liaison Officer or a Marketing/ Sales executive. Similarly, a very active person cannot fit into a purely office job. Or for that matter, a person who is too short tempered and impatient cannot make a good Teacher. Thus, every job requires certain level or combination of various personal qualities, which are reflected in your personality.

But as mentioned earlier, lack of job opportunities, stiff competition among the contestants and specialized selection procedures by the organizations have all made it difficult for you to get a job of your choice and liking. And invariably you are forced to take up any job that comes in your way whether you like it or not.

And the job you are in obviously requires certain level or combination of various personal qualities, which you may or may not possess.

You will be the luckiest person if those personal qualities, demanded of the job you are in, match with the level and combination of personal qualities you possess. It may prove to be the stepping stone to your success.

And if those personal qualities, demanded of the job you are in, do not match with the level and combination of personal qualities you possess, then you are in big trouble.

In such situations, ideally it would be better for you to identify the requirements and develop your personal qualities to suit that job. Though initially you may find it difficult to adjust yourself to the new environment, but if you could do it, in the long run you will be the happiest person. You will find pleasure in your job. You will also get job satisfaction.

On the other hand if you are not able to adjust yourself then you will have no/ less job satisfaction. You will develop less interest in your job. You may show resistance in learning about the changing rules and regulations. Your less knowledge as compared to your fellow staff will affect your performance and career.

Thus, your personality can make or mar your career.

How does it affect your Organization?

Remember, your words, actions and performance affects the name and growth of your organization.

As a 'receptionist' ideally you should possess some essential personal qualities like being well dressed with a cheerful look, courteous, a good communication skill and enough knowledge about your organization. And in the first impression itself you want to create a good impression about your company and yourself.

Whereas if you do not possess such personal qualities, in the first impression itself it can create short term damage to your organization and can affect your own career in the long run.

Similarly, a telephone operator at the company's main desk can create or damage a good impression due to lack of a good communication skill and lack of knowledge. And at times, it can even cause very serious loss of their customers and can cause substantial damage beyond imagination.

See how much damage such a job can cause to a company or organization.

Now, take the case of a 'Sales Executive'. You require a well-dressed, cheerful person with good communication and inter personal skill and with a good knowledge of their products and also about the competitive products to be able to do well for self and for the company.

Here you need some specialized skill, which of course may be a part of training. But then above all those personal qualities, you must also have a 'will to learn'. Only then you will be able to keep pace with various product developments and your competitors as well. Whereas if you lack some of those specialized skills and if you are not much interested in learning, then definitely it will affect your sales targets and also the sales growth of your company.

If you are irresponsible and non-co-operative, it can cause major problems in the working system and the overall out put / growth of the company or organization.

Working in a department for a very long period can also create plus and minus effects. Like, a person with a negative approach can loose interest in his job and make him work at a slow speed thus affecting the output.

Similarly, even at the managerial level, whether junior, middle or senior manager, if you possess those leadership qualities besides your other personal qualities, you can definitely improve the performance of your department, which can help in the progress of your career and your company. On the contrary, if you lack leadership qualities, then it can adversely affect the performance of your department thus affecting your own career and also the growth of the company.

Every career opportunity requires personal qualities at a varying level or combination to help a person to give the optimum performance level, which will directly affect his career and the organization you are working in either way.

It's only due to the failure on your part to adjust or to develop your personal qualities to suit your current profession that you become unsatisfied and look forward to a change of job fully hopping for the best. But you never know it could be more disastrous than the present one unless you are prepared to make necessary changes within you.

How do you overcome them?

You can overcome this difficulty provided you work for it and by developing and improving your personal qualities. You must have a *'WILL to improve and a WILL to work'*. Without such an attitude it's a futile exercise.

As you develop and improve your personal qualities you need to have self-control in implementing them both in your personal as well as in your professional life.

If you are sincere in your efforts then it's a matter of time. Harder you work, earlier you become successful in your efforts. You will be able to adjust / adapt yourself to any changing situation.

But there are a few other points, which will help you to prove better, say

- Dedication to your job.
- Loyalty to your organization.
- Sense of responsibility.
- Thinking of productivity.
- Avoid any personality clashes. Avoid any ego problems.
- Work as a team. Co-operate with others. Everyone is a link in your organization.
- Respect for others and believe in mutual respect. In case of any disputes, at least respect the chair.
- Never show any disparity among the staff.
- Motivate them whenever necessary. You must appreciate their good work and at the same time be firm at their mistakes.
- Do not carry your personal problems to your place of work. Concentrate in your work.
- Never work for promotion or a reward. It will come in search of you.

A good leader with weak team and strong players with a weak leader will also be able to produce good results.

****

Choose your Career

Timing for choosing your career is very important in your life.

When do you choose your Career?

Is it after you finish all your studies or much earlier? It's a question that often confuses you.

Some of you may be of the view that first you must study as much you want to and then look for a job. On the other hand, majority of you may be of the view that you must think of it much earlier and then plan your studies.

Let's take the first case. You want to finish your studies and then look for a career opportunity. Want to finish your studies? What kind of studies and in which field? What should be the level of your studies? What kind of a career will you get then?

Here, since there is no specific idea about your future and about the kind of career you want to choose, you will generally be guided by the educational facilities that are available around you.

You will again be limited by the higher education that are offered in the colleges and universities and you may not bother about the credibility of the courses you are doing and the about the institutions you are studying.

Under such circumstances, you have not pursued in your field of interest. You have not stretched your imagination about your future prospects and undertaken your higher studies / professional studies or specialization.

At the end of your education, which may or may not fetch you a good job, you are out in the open and will be searching for a job that can match whatever educational qualification you have.

Whereas in the second case, you set up an ambition much earlier in your life getting inspiration, it could be from your own parents, friends or others. You must also have some self-motivation that you want to become someone in life, to do well in life and you may have your 'field of interest'.

Here, you have a definite goal to achieve and you know how to achieve that goal. Accordingly, you plan your studies. You will be very particular and choosy about your higher studies and field of specialization. Even you will be very careful in selecting the college and the university where you want to pursue your studies; because after your studies when you look for a career, the companies and the recruiters look not only for your qualification but also at the college and the universities from where you have obtained those qualifications.

You will put in your hard work and try to excel in your studies. It will help you to score a higher grading and this will get you to the top of the merit list while applying for a job.

Once while giving a talk to the senior students of a public school, I conducted a small exercise. In a specially prepared format I told them to write down their name, class, details of parents if working.

They were also asked to write about 'What their parents wanted them to become?' and 'What they wanted to become and why?' And they were assured that the information would be kept confidential.

At the end of the exercise the result was quite amazing. In about 30 % of the cases, the ambitions of the students and their parents were the same. Here, it is quite possible that the children wanted to follow the wishes and desire of their parents or rather they wanted to fulfill the expectations of their parents about them or they are not fully aware of various career opportunities opened to them.

In another 35 % of the cases, the ambition of the students and their parents differed. Here, some of the parents wanted their children to follow their own profession / business line or any other profession, which they felt are good and will give a bright future for their children. But their children may be interested in careers that would provide them a better future, better career prospects and better job satisfaction, especially in this new world of new Information Technology. It only reflects lack of understanding and interaction between the parents and their children. And it's a matter of concern.

But what surprised me were the balance 35 % cases where the parents had no particular ambition or expectations about their children and had left the choice entirely to their children. This case is a matter of deep concern. Here, either the parents are unable to help their children in choosing a suitable career or they may not possessing enough knowledge for giving proper career guidance to their children.

In a way in such cases, may be those parents wanted to give a free hand in deciding the future of their children. But they should not forget that their children need to be guided about various career opportunities and their plus and minus points. This will help the children to exercise their mind and be able to set a realistic ambition in their life.

Or maybe they don't want to take the responsibility in shaping the future of their children or may be that they don't want to be blamed for anything that may go wrong in pursuing a career. And most of children in this category had no idea about their future plan or set an ambition in their life.

How to choose the 'Right Path'?

Now the choice is yours, i.e. either you develop and strengthen those qualities for your chosen career or change your career option to suit your personality.

It is always preferred to set an ambition in your life, choose a career of your liking and then work towards that goal than being contented with what is available to you.

Remember a strong will power and tremendous self-confidence can take you anywhere you want to, provided you work for it.

Check List

Here is a Check List, which will help you to select a suitable career.

- *Your Ambition,*
- *Evaluate of your 'Personal Qualities',*
- *Identify the career opportunities that suit your personality,*
- *Your Qualification or the qualification you must possess,*
- *Your 'Physical and Mental Strength',*

- *Support from your parents / family members,*
- *Your views about 'Family Life',*
- *Growth and education of your children,*
- *Job transfers and how do they affect the growth of your children and family life?*
- *Prospects for promotion,*
- *Will it provide you enough financial security?*

After evaluation of all the above points, you must choose a career that suits you best and your needs and you must work towards in that direction.

Specialization and the Institution

After you have chosen a suitable career path you should pursue your studies accordingly. It's here you should think of further specialization in your proposed field of activity and the institution where you should do your specialization.

Specialisation in your proposed field of activity can always boost your knowledge and brighten your career prospects. You can do your specialisation either before taking up a career itself or after gaining some work experience or even you could think of doing your specilisation while pursuing your career. It will depend upon the career you have chosen and your self-confidence and determination in pursuing a better career prospect.

An important point to note here is about the institute where you want to pursue your higher studies and specialisation. Institute matters a lot in providing 'quality education', which will help you to get a better career.

Various factors that you should look for while selecting an institution for your higher studies / specialisation are its academic excellence, overall development it provides, its 'placement record' of the passed out students and its acceptance at the domestic as well as in the international level.

While it will be difficult to get admission to such renowned institutions, bright and intelligent students can always find their way there and also grab various scholarships that are offered and available for the deserving students.

Career Guidance

As mentioned earlier, the fast growing Science and Information Technology are really making tremendous progress and changes in our life style beyond imagination. Though it has opened up new chapters in career opportunities, the younger generation today find themselves in quite a confused state of mind in grooming themselves to take on the challenges ahead of them and in selecting a suitable career path and pursuing their higher and professional studies. The information and guidance they get from their parents and surroundings are often felt inadequate.

It's here you feel the necessity and importance of a career guidance. Though many institutions provide a talk or a programme on career guidance to their students, you are also advised to make reference to some books on career guidance and or go for career guidance counseling. It has always proved to be very useful and effective.

During a number of programmes given to various college and Plus One and Two students, I had always felt their knowledge, on various career opportunities available to them, was much less than expected. And I found them to most attentive and interested in listening to such career guidance programmes.

A large number of students often changed their earlier ambition to a new and a better ambition after listening to such programmes. And most amazing thing was that number of students who did not have any ambition in their life, or those who had not yet decided about their ambition, had set their ambition after such programmes.

A proper insight to various career opportunities must be given to the students at their Plus Two / Pre Degree levels during their first year itself, so that the students are able to choose a suitable career path and pursue their further higher and professional studies.

A similar programme should also be conducted during the later years of their higher / professional studies so that they are able to refresh their knowledge, which will help them to select a suitable career.

Work-Life Balance

It is hard sometimes to draw the line between our career and personal lives when the lines blur so much with our own work. In order to be your best at work it is important to find balance in your career and personal life.

We have a few tips to help you work through the struggle of balancing your career with your life outside of the office.

- Define work time and personal time.
- Separate your work life and personal life as much as possible.
- Work smarter, not harder
- Leave work at work
- Set your own rules

There is no doubt that finding a balance can be hard, but it is possible. With some important boundaries, you can find a healthy life outside of your office doors.

****

Career Opportunities

Traditional vocations and careers give away a host of new opportunities to the new generation. However, possessing knowledge and the ability to add on to the existing knowledge is going to be the source of power in tomorrow's organizations and individuals.

The cumulative effect of automation, liberalization, privatization and globalization has transformed the Indian job market. *It's not that the existing job opportunities are shrinking but it's the nature of the jobs or work that is changing.* In fact, now there is a lot of work, interesting, challenging, creative and highly satisfying. It's for you to equip yourself with what is needed to qualify for those exciting job opportunities.

In the organized sectors jobs are getting scarcer but new and glamorous job opportunities are emerging with unrealistic figures as remuneration packages for knowledge-workers. With the bulk of job employment showing an upward trend in the unorganized sector, future job aspirants have to gear up for the challenges. From a strong foundation in your speciality you can branch out in many directions as required by the changing circumstances. The higher qualified and experienced will be able to quote their price in the job market.

The situation has never been better but the sense of insecurity has become stronger. The future belongs to those people who are specialized in specific job skills. The acquisition of knowledge and skills therefore, will be of greater importance than ever before.

Each career demands at least some level of personal qualities / personality for giving the best output / performance expected of that career.

Therefore, you should have a general awareness of various career opportunities that are available so that you are able to plan your career.

You have career opportunities within your country and abroad.

Career Opportunities within the Country

Career opportunities within the country are under the Central / State Govt. departments/ organizations, in the Private Sector organizations / undertakings and as Entrepreneurs.

Within these areas, there are different career fields that you can choose depending upon your taste, qualification and ambition.

The selection/ recruitment to the Central/ State Govt. departments/ Undertakings are done by the Union Public Service Commission (UPSC) / State Public Service Commission (PSC) / central/ state employment exchanges, through a thorough selection procedure, whereas in the Private Sector, the selection / recruitment of candidates are done as per their requirement through their own selection procedures.

Different career fields that exist are mentioned below.

Central/ State Govt. Depts. /Organizations

At the Central and various State Governments of our country, we have different Ministries like, Finance, Health, Education, Industry, Commerce, Agriculture, Public Works, Forest, Law, Transport, Petroleum and Chemicals, Revenue, Railways, Human Rights and Social Welfare, Communications, Science and Technology, External Affairs, Home Affairs, Parliamentary Affairs, etc.

Under each Ministry, there are innumerous job opportunities at various levels, from the higher level executives in the Indian Civil Services to the lower level of jobs.

While the Armed Forces like army, navy and airforce, border security forces and other central security forces come under the purview of the central government, other security forces are under the control of the state governments.

They provide innumerable job opportunities both at the officer rank level and below the officer rank and include both technical and non-technical areas, in all most in all categories one could think off.

Educational Field

Over the years, there have been tremendous reforms and changes in the field of education to meet the growing challenges of the future in matching with the outside world. The education system of our country is always matching with some of the best education systems in the world today.

Teaching regarded as a noble profession plays a major role in 'shaping the younger generation of our country'. From kindergarten to the highest level of the education system today, offer ample career opportunities to the dedicated professionals.

Under the existing educational system whether government or the private sector, there are plenty of job opportunities like, vice chancellors, registrars, principals, readers, professors, lecturers, headmasters, school teachers, library staff, lab assistants, clerks, attendant, peon, watchman and so on.

Depending upon your interest, you can get a job under the government or the private sector based on your educational qualifications and subject to your selection through their selection procedures.

Science and Technology

Being a developing country more thrust is given for the development of science and technology. And this has taken our country to the front line of the developing nations.

Mostly the science and technology departments are under the control of the central government, there are also certain institutions and organizations under the control of state governments and in the private sector.

They provide job opportunities not only for high tech people in the sense people with high qualification both in science and engineering and but also for others in various categories.

It's a field highly suited for those who are looking for high tech jobs, who are very much interested in research and development works and looking for exciting results, who are really intelligent and are keen to work and put in their best for the development of the country.

For more information about careers in the field of Science and Technology, please refer to the section 'Selected Professions'-Science and Technology.

Healthcare Services

'A healthy mind in a healthy body' is a good old saying. One may have a healthy mind. But without a healthy body we cannot do a thing. Therefore, we consider protection of human lives as the most important thing in this world; thus, the importance of 'Healthcare Services'.

Besides the Healthcare Services available under the Central/ State governments, the growth in the number of health clinics, nursing homes, hospitals, specialist hospitals and other healthcare services in the private sector has been tremendous and beyond words.

Compared to the olden days, the increasing awareness of healthcare programmes coupled with introduction of modern and sophisticated diagnostic instruments and equipment paved the way for this fast growth in this field.

It has also given birth to a number of new specialized branches of healthcare. Further, use of ultra modern diagnostic instruments and equipment's, have created the need for highly specialized technicians and engineers in medical electronics.

Caring the aged, mentally retarded physically handicapped and the poor has also received very significant attention. Today we find a number of organizations, more in the private sector, engaged in such noble activities. These are institutions and organizations, which are mostly self-contained with full infrastructure.

In addition, 'Medical Transcription' is another new area, which has come up in the healthcare services of certain countries and this has created employment opportunities for a large number of 'Medical Transcriptionist'.

Thus, there are innumerable employment opportunities available in the field of 'Healthcare Services'. Also refer to the section 'Selected Professions- Medical' for more information.

Agriculture

Though agricultural ministries under the central and state governments provide vast employment opportunities, agriculture in the private sector also provide similar employment opportunities.

Primarily it is cultivation of land and rearing of animals. But with the advancement of science and technology it has spread its wings to more specialized activities like horticulture, floriculture and aquaculture.

With the advancement of science and technology, there has been a tremendous improvement in the field of agriculture in the method of cultivation, like use of hybrid seeds, chemical fertilizers, pesticides, agro-equipment, harvesting and preservation of crops.

Further, the new branch of studies, the biotechnology, has strengthened the scope for further rapid advancement in the field of agriculture. Through crop rotation, a multiple crop cultivation has helped to facilitate commercial cultivation for both domestic and international markets.

In order to cope up the developments achieved in the developed countries, new courses of instructions are included in the present agricultural education system, which makes the new generation more specialized in the field of agriculture. And thus it provides more career opportunities.

The help and guidance provided through the media and the encouragement given by various organizations have further attracted more entrepreneurs into this field.

Also refer to the Section on 'Selected Professions – Agriculture' for more information.

Industry

Industry is the backbone for the growth of any country, especially so in a developing country and it's an accepted fact. Though a number of large and critical industrial units are in the public sector, it won't be wrong to put on record that the industrial growth of our country is controlled by the industries in the private sector. You name any industry in any field and you have it here in our country.

In the recent years, due to the advancement of science and technology and transfer of high technology, the industrial products of our country have achieved very high quality standards matching the international quality standards. Today our country's products are considered at par with some of the best products available in the international markets. And the credit goes to the technological progress, quality management and the dedicated industrial workforce.

Over the years, there has been a drastic change in the outlook, method, functioning, and product standards. Thanks to the technological advancement and 'will' to excel and a desire to be 'second to none'.

Thus industry has opened innumerable employment opportunities for people in different field of activities and at various levels, whether non-technical or technical, highly qualified or less qualified and with or without specialization.

It also provides as a platform for those upcoming entrepreneurs and young industrialists to make a beginning of their own.

Also refer to the Section on 'Selected Professions – Science and Technology' for more information.

Information Technology (IT)

We are moving on from the industrial revolution through an 'Internet revolution', a digital age in a way. Electronics and telecommunication has been the foundation of the Internet Revolution.

Information Technology is the collective term used for various technologies involved in processing and transmitting information. And they include computing, telecommunications and microelectronics.

Some of the software packages like word processing, database, spreadsheets etc. have really revolutionized the office working systems. Not only can work be done more quickly and efficiently than before, but IT has given the 'decision makers' the opportunity to consider far more data than before, before taking their decisions.

Today, software developers, network engineers, system administrators, computer programmers, system programmers and system analysts, database managers, and system security specialists etc. are in great demand.

While a BE / B Tech. in Computer Engineering or Computer Science & Engineering or Information Technology or MCA are best preferred for these jobs, other basic engineering courses/ Post Graduate/ Graduate courses plus additional long and short courses in the computer field, also makes you suitable for various employment opportunities in the areas of Information Technology.

Actually, there is virtually no end to the courses offered in Information Technology. *It's important for an aspiring IT professional to understand their individual strength, their own assessment to find where they fit in the best and then undertake focused training.*

It's not that the best opportunities are only in becoming software developers. In the present age of 'Internet Revolution', there are golden opportunities in the areas connected with Internet like Web Designers, Web Developers, Web Content providers, Web Master etc.

Web Designers are expected to be proficient in their respective areas. Apart from aesthetic sense and awareness of information architecture a web designer should build familiarity with computer based design tools. A good web designer is also expected to have awareness of scripting languages.

Web Developers ensure that a site is fully functional. They should know relevant scripting languages including dynamic HTML. Even they are expected to have XML knowledge.

Websites need content, which has to be appealing and precise. Therefore, in order to become a website content provider, you have to acquire these skills and the basic knowledge and information on whichever topic or field you are writing.

Webmaster is the pivot of the website. As webmaster you are responsible for everything on the site. To become a webmaster you require all the skills of the web designer, web developer, and the content provider with good managerial and communication skills.

In addition to these, innumerable job opportunities are also available in other areas like E-Commerce, Multimedia, Entertainment and Communications. You require specialized qualification and training for working in these specialized areas and the most satisfying fact is that facility for such specialized and professional training are also available on our country.

Research and development, computing, inventory management, quality control, accounting, personal administration, recruitment, secretarial, marketing, advertising, distribution and legal services are required in all economic sectors. Information Technology has enabled the outsourcing of these activities. India is already in a strong position as an important global for some of these services.

The latest to attract in this field is Medical Transcription where medical records of medical consultants in dicta-phones are being transcribed.

In the highly technology-oriented work environment, there is greater demand for good repairs, mechanics, maintenance and other technical support services also.

Anything connected with Information Technology witness rapid changes. And that is why no one can ever predict accurately. The job profiles can change totally in a short span of a few months to one year due to the evolving technologies.

When it comes to the knowledge and skills for careers in the field of Internet, Multimedia, Communications or in fact in any field connected to Information Technology directly or indirectly, the 'Survival Rule' will be, 'to master the knowledge and basic skills and keep track of all the new developments connected to your field of activity'.

Having crossed the boundaries of physical laws, Information Technology continues to expand in unforeseen directions and so do the career opportunities.

Business / Commerce

All business activities including banking are important and essential fields of activities the human race need. Over the centuries, the business style has been changing as per the progress made in the field of science and technology. It stretched from a local market to wider markets at national and the trade crossed the national boundaries to enter into international levels.

It was the beginning of a new era and it found more career opportunities in the domestic as well as in the international market. The industrial growth coupled with the progress of science and technology brought tremendous upward changes and immense growth in domestic and international business activities.

Now, further advancement in the field of science and technology and the industrial revolution, have paved the way for the highly sophisticated Information Technology. And this highly expanding field of Information Technology and the Internet revolution has given birth to a totally new concept of trading, an electronic commerce or most popularly known E-Commerce.

E-Commerce / E-Business is a trading or business activity conducted using the electronic media, new methods of communication, marketing, transaction, delivery of materials and payment systems and follow ups.

E-Commerce is also expected to open innumerable job opportunities. Being in its initial stages E-commerce is expected to make substantial changes in its approach and actual business operations. And therefore, one need to have a thorough knowledge about E-commerce and be prepared to adapt to further change that will bring in, before you decide to make a career in this field.

Here, computer professionals handle the technical set up, while marketing, advertising, management and accounting professionals are in great demand to run the business.

Web marketing requires professionals who are able to convince advertisers that the site has lot of traffic, which will ensure that they will get the value of their money by putting their advertisement on the site or sponsors some sections of the site. Though general marketing skills and knowledge for any other media are good enough, some employers also insist on some technical knowledge to appreciate the working of the medium.

To become an expert on handling the E-commerce technicalities and technologies, it's better to be a computer professional with sufficient knowledge in this field.

Media World

We use the media to convey our ideas, feelings and other news to others across the world, which are Print media, Audio and Visual media. And they, Newspaper, Weekly, Magazines, Radio, TV, Advertising, publishing etc. no doubt, play the key role for the success of almost every field of activities.

News reporters, freelance writers, journalists, photographer, proof readers, artists, vishualiser, computer professionals, models and other technicians and staff in the field of publishing are the areas where one can hopefully look forward for a number of job opportunities.

Now, the technological progress and the 'Internet Revolution' have really made revolutionary changes to every field of the media world. In a way it has brought in a new concept of technology and in the approach to the audience/ mass.

Even editorial staff from the print media are moving to on-line magazines, various portals and websites. While opportunities in journalism will continue to be in demand, Information Technology enabled journalists are likely to be more in demand. Though the core competency will not change, the delivery mechanism will change in this Internet world and therefore, they would be better off learning Web authoring and Web publishing tools or graphics and media tools.

Multimedia is a growing field with tremendous job potential. Multimedia is the ability to capture, store, manipulate, transfer and display multiple media such as text, numbers, graphics, audio, video, and animation on computer exploring its inter active skills. It is produced in both, offline format or CD and online format for the Internet Webpage. *Creative skills and training will be helpful for excelling in multimedia.*

Some of the specialized areas are graphics handling including computer-aided art and painting, digital photography, scanning, desktop publishing, colour printing, font design, lay out design etc. In audio handling there is digitalization of speech, music and sound, audio compression, sound synthesis, speech processing etc. and video handling involves video imaging technology, audio synchronization, image compression, and designing of codes, which codes video images into bytes and again decodes the bytes back into video images.

The areas of work in this multimedia will be in desktop publishing, advertising, corporate communication and Web designing.

There are plenty of careers in all areas of electronic media production, direction, delivery and in technological.

Entertainment

When we think of 'entertainment' straight thoughts that come to you are about cinema and music and dance? But the advancement of science and technology brought many changes. This gave a tremendous boost to the film industry as well as to other various fields of the entertainment world. *Keeping people informed and entertained is a big business today.*

The film industry has plenty of job opportunities like in acting, direction, photography, make up, costume designer, visualizer, story writer, script writer, set designer, editing, audio and video technicians and a row of other assistants.

The storming wave of the Information Technology has really made sweeping changes in the entertainment world in terms of the use of technology and in quality. The 'special effects' with the use of computer gave a further boost to the film industry.

India is becoming an important entertainment hub. The unlimited growth of Information Technology also brought unimaginable advancement in television technology. There is a huge swell in entertainment channels and today, it is the fastest growth area.

There are more cartoons, music videos today than before. Therefore, there is a great demand for announcers, anchors, performers, singers, directors, producers, newsreaders/ anchors, television journalists, photographers, cinematographers, art directors, set designers, costume/ fashion designers etc. for the ever growing television channels.

Television technology has become a household necessity and now that it has been hitched to the information revolution it is becoming interactive, digitized, and it is quickly evolving as an essential tool for the new century. The global trend of convergence is becoming a reality in India.

You must get trained professionally in Mass Communication, Journalism, Television, Film, Drama, Music or Dance etc. Learning on the job through trainee-ship is one way to carve out a niche.

Sports and Games

Even in this world of advanced science and technology, sports and games play an important role in the human life. If it is for a mere entertainment for the majority, it is the breadwinner for many.

Progress in the field of science and technology brought in many changes in the conventional methods, whether it was the equipment, practice or execution. Invention of new modern sports gear and equipment really made changes in quality and helped the participants to better their performance.

New games and sports events and more organized sports and games meets gave more opportunities to the younger generation to take more interest in this field and even to accept it as their career in their life.

Those lucky ones, their outstanding performances really earned them national and international recognition and are virtually become the heroes of today.

Therefore, the field of sports and games is not an area to be neglected at all. Those who have the physical strength, talent, self-confidence and determination should definitely opt for this field and make a good career for themselves. And it is for their parents and guardians to give them full support and encourage them in their efforts.

Further, field of sports and games has given great openings for entrepreneurs to find their success in setting up industries for the manufacture of sports gear and games kit and equipment and in their business.

This field offers tremendous career opportunities as participants, referees, umpires, coach, commentators, and a lot of other categories connected with this field.

Social Service

A number of social service institutes and organisations under the control of the central and various state governments are taking care of the needy, poor, old, orphans, physically handicapped and mentally retarded. And various job opportunities are included under the central and state government career opportunities.

The increasing awareness for the 'need for human consideration' has really made the people to set up a large number of similar institutes and organizations in the private sector. And today we have a very large number of such institutes and organizations all over our country.

And these institutes and organizations require a lot of people with specialized training or otherwise who are willing to take care of the inmates and to run such institutes, with and without remuneration. Services of people from every walk of life can be absorbed in these areas. Working in these field gives more of mental peace apart from the job satisfaction.

Further it also provides challenges and opportunities for the genius to put their heart and soul in finding solutions to individual or common problems of such affected personnel, whether it is artificial limbs/ other instruments or gadgets for the physically handicapped, innovative systems for helping the mentally retarded and for others.

Political

What? Does politics have a good career opportunity? Why not? Like in any other field, politics also has plenty of career opportunities at various levels.

India is the biggest democratic country in the world today, where we have a government of the people, by the people and for the people. Successful regional and national political parties govern the country. And each political party has its own functional organization with numerous portfolios, which are often filled by efficient leaders and members of their parties.

The elected political party / parties form the governments at the state and at the Centre. And all the ministers from the post of the prime minister, cabinet and other ministerial posts at the central government to the chief ministers, cabinet and other ministerial posts at the state level governments are all selected from the elected members of the political parties. Further, all those elected members to the parliament as well as to the state assemblies belong to various political parties, who also enjoy a considerable amount of salary / allowances, perks and other privileges.

So why not try your luck too! Become a good politician and then become active and efficient to be nominated as a candidate for the election and later get selected to higher positions in the country's governing body.

But remember, as the growing citizen of tomorrow you must dedicate yourself to the nation. You should be self-confident, determined and be prepared to work for the up lift of your motherland giving emphasis to social harmony and welfare of the people.

This is what the society and our motherland expects from you.

Religious

Mostly you find people work to make their own living comfortable. Some, though giving priority for their own living comforts, also spent some time and efforts for caring the 'needy'. But there are some people and some sections of the society who forgo own comforts in life and work for others.

They offer their dedicated services to teach about the good things in life, make them understand 'values of human life', providing them physical, mental and spiritual health and guide and help them to 'live and let live', to make a world free from hatred and violence.

These are the religious institutions and organizations offering various career openings for you at various levels of their activities with and without remuneration. So the choice is yours whether you want to serve the people or you want to make a career for yourself elsewhere.

****

Application, CV / Résumé

Unemployment has been a major problem in our country since our independence and it is increasing day by day. With lesser job opportunities as compared to the ever-growing number of job seekers, it is becoming more and more difficult for the younger generation to get a job. Therefore, it has become all the more important for you to take immediate and proper action in hunting for job; the earlier the better. Any delay in taking a proper and prompt action will mean others taking over your rare golden opportunity.

Though there are different methods for screening candidates, examination of an applicant's track record combined with an interview assessment still remain the traditional way of selection.

Application

An application is a formal request for anything. Your application can be made in two ways, in your own written letter form or fill in the one that is already printed and supplied by the employer.

In case of your own written application, make a draft, check and ensure it contains everything that you wanted to convey about yourself (Bio-data) to the employer. Get it checked by someone who you think can help you and trust. Preferably type it in a computer so that you could carry out corrections / alterations if any, later on. This would also help you when making several applications around the same time. Make sure that your handwriting is easy to read and there are no spelling mistakes. You must sign the letter at the bottom and write your name below your signature.

In most of the cases, you apply for a job in a printed form. If it is a printed form, fill it carefully. You may fill it with your own hand if possible or else type it. You must know the reason why the employer has given you a printed application form. By doing so they are able to compare one application with another. Therefore, you must fill in all columns of the application as far as possible and avoid giving any remarks in any of the columns as 'Refer to CV'. This will require the reader some extra efforts to understand your application.

An application normally contains the following-
- Surname, full name and address- temporary/ permanent.
- Date of birth/ place of birth.
- Marital status.
- Details of parent, Guardian with their address.
- Nationality.
- Religion.
- Details of education and other qualifications.
- Details of your previous employment / experience.
- Health.
- Hobbies and other interests.
- References if any.

An application is an important document and is regarded as confidential, specially so, until the applicant is interviewed. This saves an embarrassment to the applicant of letting his employer know that he/she is seeking a job somewhere else.

If your application is for a particular job, and if you don't make the grade, then you loose your chance. Whereas if your application is for a particular job with a mention 'or any other suitable job', you may also be considered for any other suitable job based on your qualifications.

For a fresh job seeker, fresh from Xth standard/ Plus Two/ Degree/ or any other professional courses, making up a good track record is quite difficult since they may not have much or any experience. Even under such circumstances you must mention your other areas of interest and activities under the heading 'Hobbies and other interests' like, as a house captain, school leader/ chairman of the college union, your organizing ability, interpersonal skills, computer knowledge, typing and shorthand, any part-time activities if any or any other personal achievements. Some of them indicate your 'leadership qualities'. All these may add to your personal qualities, which an employer will consider for other useful employability in the company. Thus, you gain an edge over other candidates with similar qualifications for a particular job.

A *reference* is always kept confidential. Generally, you are allowed to give the names of two referees in your application. You must select someone who knows you well enough to be able to be reliable to anybody dealing with your application. Preferably, they must be of good standing, in your own interest, who can give an unprejudiced appraisal of you. And of course, this must be done with their permission.

But before you send your application, you must read the advertisement and description of the job very carefully and then make sure that you really want the job you are applying for.

If there are more than one job opportunities coming up at the same time, you must apply to all of them without any fear instead of waiting for the result from one company. And you must try to accept your first better opportunity that comes in.

Here is a **Check list** for preparing your application.

- Read the advertisement and description of the job very carefully and then make sure that you really want the job you are applying for.
- Does your qualifications match the job requirement you are applying for?
- In case of a hand written, write it on a A4 sheet with proper margins.
- Have you filled in the application form fully and correctly?
- Is your handwriting legible and easy to read?
- Make sure your application contains everything that you wanted to convey about yourself to the employer.
- As far as possible give the details of two *Referees*.
- Keep your certificates ready all the time.
- Always enclose your passport size photograph, whether asked for or not, it could be an omission.
- Write down the employment/ job reference code on the application and on the envelope or as directed by the employer.

Curriculum Vitaé (CV) / Résumé

Curriculum Vitae is a brief account of somebody's previous career, usually submitted along with an application for a job. While the term 'Curriculum Vitaé' is used in UK and in some other countries, another term 'Résumé' is used for the same purpose in US and in a number of other countries. However, the term 'Curriculum Vitaé' is more commonly and widely used term.

In the case of lower and middle employment opportunities, submission of written applications or filled in application forms supplied by the employer are considered adequate for the selection of suitable candidates. Whereas, for higher employment opportunities the employer need to know as much relevant information as possible about the candidates so that they are able to pick and choose the *best* for their requirement.

In the present world scenario, where the science and technology is progressing at such a fast rate almost beyond our imagination and in a highly competitive world, such relevant information has become a usual thing that every employer is looking for. Therefore, there is a need for applying for a job in such a format, especially so when applying for a higher employment opportunity, so that your case stands out and the employer is able to identify you as 'special' as compared to other applicants. This is where the CV (Curriculum Vitaé) comes into play.

A good CV (Curriculum Vitaé) makes a lot of difference in everything and it can even change your fortune. At the same time a badly prepared CV can undersell you disastrously, offering them less information about you and it can ruin your excellent career opportunity in spite of your high qualification and experience. Therefore, it is all the more important that you realise the importance of a well prepared CV.

This book will provide you with an easy-to-follow guide for the preparation of a CV. It is well understood that a CV is prepared for a person to suit his personal details, education and qualifications, work experience and other interests. Thus, every CV will differ from others in one way or other. And it is next to impossible to describe or give samples of such a large number of CVs with lots of permutations and combinations. However, simple mechanics of preparation of a standard CV with lots of explanations and suggestions will definitely help you to write an appropriate CV for yourselves and for others.

A CV has two parts, the first part contains *Personal Details* and the second part contains *Curriculum Vitaé*, which further includes *Education and Qualification, Training, Experience* and at the end *Other Activities*.

Personal Details

It should provide all your personal details that an employer will be interested to know and therefore, it should preferably include,

Full Name	: xxxxx
Occupation	: Nil (In case already working give the name of the profession)
Address	: xxxxxx
Telephone No	: xxxxxx
Date of Birth	: xxxxxx
Place of Birth	: xxxxxx
Nationality	: xxxxxx
Religion	: xxxxxx
Marital Status	: xxxxxx
Next of Kin	: xxxxxx
Passport No	: xxxxxx
Driving License	: xxxxxx
Health	: xxxxxx

However, persons not possessing a driving license or a passport need not include them. Similarly, if you are a disabled person, then you should mention about your disability whether such disability will affect the job you have applied for or not. This will increase your job prospects in the general stream and under the 'disabled quota' if they have a quota for disabled persons.

Education and Qualification

This section will vary from person to person based on the education and qualifications. Generally, your education from Xth standard onwards are included in an ascending order, which means that you start with your details from Xth standard onwards then Plus Two/ Pre-degree, degree, Post-graduation and so on. The details should include name of the school or college or institution, place, the education and qualification you have obtained from there, grade and the year of passing.

If you are able to take some part-time courses/ qualifications along with your main stream of studies, then you may add them at the appropriate place with a mention that they are qualifications, which require part-time attendance only. This will clarify the matter in case of any doubt or confusion.

If you have gained some additional qualification by doing additional courses, they must be given in detail separately under the heading 'Qualification', thus splitting into Education followed by Qualification.

Training

Industrial placements or college placements for whatever duration should be treated as a normal job in the career history. Similarly, many applicants may have attended short or long training programmes run by their employing company or by some other specialized training organizations. Since such things will have a bearing on your future employment opportunities you must include them in your CV.

If the applicant is a member of any professional association, then it should also be mentioned.

Experience

Experience, in other words 'career history', forms the major and interesting part of your CV. It requires a very major effort. It speaks of your past professional activities, achievements and your professional competence, which will help your employment opportunity.

Details of your experience are given in a descending order, i.e. it should read backwards. And there is a reason for it. The employer will be interested to know about your recent assignments and performance.

The details should include your experience covering a period of last ten years, if you have a long service and may be even more if you are applying for a very senior/ higher job, which requires much longer service or experience.

You should give the name of your employer, their business activity, your assignment/ job responsibilities, period of employment and your achievements and highlighting some of your outstanding achievements if any. You may have held different appointments in the same company. In such cases, you must specify each appointment with duration and your achievements in each assignment. This will give a clear picture of your progressive career and about your future employability.

If there is a break in your service, you must mention it clearly, whether it was on some medical grounds, or for gaining some additional qualifications, which the employer could verify from your 'Education and Qualification' section.

For fresh candidates, who are seeking for a job for the first time can give their 'Part-time work experience' if they have while they were studying, like some weekend jobs, evening jobs etc. In such cases, the career history need not be given in the reverse order.

Please note that while giving out your career history, you should never mention about the salary you had drawn in your earlier employment unless the advertisement requests you to mention about your salary last drawn. This will only harm your prospects.

Other Activities

Under this heading you generally include about your 'Hobbies', the languages you can speak/read and write, and about the 'References' you want to give.

About your hobbies, give only those hobbies in which you are really interested. It is an area, which reflects on your personal character. Never give names of some hobbies for the heck of it. It will only put you in trouble at the time of your interview.

Give the details of the 'Referees' as mentioned earlier. Or else you could even mention as 'Available on request'. Though in certain cases this may suffice, in case of higher jobs, it is better that you give the details of your 'Referees' for your own benefit.

Here is a **Check list** on preparation of CV (Curriculum Vitaé)

- Ensure your CV has all the sections as described above.

- Does the Personal Details Section include all essential information?
- Have you given full and correct details in Education and Qualification Section?
- Is it in an ascending order?
- Have you given your 'Qualification' separately?
- Have you given the details of your 'Training' fully?
- Are you a member of any professional association? If so have you given the details?
- Have you given necessary details of your 'Experience' (career history) in the CV?
- If so, is it in a descending order?
- Does it include your pervious employer's name, their business activities, your-designation and job responsibilities with period, your achievements if any?
- Do not mention about your earlier drawn salary unless asked for.
- Have you given information under 'Other Activities', like your hobbies, languages known, and about the details of your 'Referees'?
- Prepare your CV on A4 size sheets with the help of a computer if possible.
- Your CV ideally should not be more than 2 to 4 pages.
- Do not try to reduce the number of pages by using small types and reduced margins.
- Send copies of your passport size photograph as asked for by the employer and in case it is not asked for, you may send one of your passport size photographs.

Though there may be different views about the layout of a CV, the suggested layout and the method of preparing a CV are of the standard acceptable to any employers including highly professional employers.

Your CV must always be accompanied by an introductory letter. Remember, the standard of that letter is as important as your CV.

Applicants those who have a good CV may fail to get an 'interview call' because of a bad introductory letter. This letter creates an impression and an impressive letter can even overcome the odd weakness in a CV. Similarly, a poor letter could cause in an outright rejection of a good CV.

The letter should be short, crisp and clear. It should mention the date of issue of publication of the advertisement with the job reference number/ code if any. You should then say that you are very much interested in the job and that you have the requisite education, qualification and experience for the same and may mention about your availability for a personal interview. And the letter should be addressed to the right person as mentioned in their advertisement.

****

Interview

An 'Interview' is a 'meeting at which questions are asked by the interviewer to get some information or to find out the suitability of a person for a particular purpose.

Type of Interviews

Generally, interviews can be grouped under the following categories:

- **Interviews for Educational purposes**. This may be for admission of children at the beginning of their schooling, for admission to higher studies/ professional courses, 'viva' i.e. the oral examination conducted by the universities for Post Graduation and Doctoral studies and for granting / awarding scholarships.
- **Job Interviews:** These types of interviews are conducted with a view to select suitable candidates for filling the vacancies in an establishment or organization. They could be 'simple interviews' conducted for simple and average jobs and 'highly professional interviews' for highly technical and professional jobs.
- **Interviews for 'Promotion'**: Every establishment or organization will have its own promotion policies. While promotions up to certain level are based on the length of your service and the 'annual confidential reports/ annual performance reports, further promotions may be based on your length of service, your annual report, internal promotional examinations and a personal interview at the end, especially for the posts coming under 'selection grade'. By doing so, the employees are given an opportunity to prove their worth and more efficient individuals are selected to occupy senior/ higher positions. This also helps to improve the employer's functional efficiency.

- **Special Interviews:** for some specific purposes. These are interviews conducted on some special occasions for a specific purpose. For e.g. an interview of a political figure by a reporter, an interview of a celebrity, interview of some persons by their organisations for selecting an outstanding candidate for assigning some very important and critical tasks or to select an appropriate personality for heading an important project work, or may be to select someone for a prestigious foreign assignment, or may be for selecting the most deserving personality for a prestigious award and on other similar occasions.

Further, if the number of eligible candidates is more for interview, then the process of selection is conducted in a different way. In the first phase, in a 'preliminary interview' suitable candidates are 'short listed' thus reducing the number of candidates for the final selection. And during the 'final interview', the final selection of the candidates is made.

Whatever be the type and the style of interview, you must be able to make an impact on the interviewer.

What makes a Good Interview?

A good interview is the one where a candidate achieves a 'rapport' with the interviewer. The candidate will be able to leave the room with full satisfaction that he/she is able to put in the best and perform well at the interview. The candidate will have sufficient confidence in the interviewer to feel sure that the successful candidate must deserve the success.

And the interviewer gets a feeling that he/she is able to interview the candidate deeply enough to decide to select the 'best' of the lot.

A job interview may be conducted by a single person or by a group of persons; all depended on the size of the establishment/ organization and the level of the job.

This section of the book discusses *'Job Interview'*, and contains very useful information and interview techniques for those on their job hunting and those who are in the process of thinking for a suitable change of job.

No interview is similar; because no candidate is like any other; their qualification, experience, knowledge and personal qualities all differ from each other.

Why Preparation is so important?

It is a process where the best is chosen from the available lot. And, the way you present yourself at the interview, the way you express yourself, the way you react to certain situation, everything from the beginning till the end matters. Therefore, you cannot take a risk of being casual or ignorant about your interview. It may cost you very dearly.

The most disappointment will be when a person who possess all the basic qualifications, experience, knowledge and enough personal qualities to make him a prospective candidate, loses the chance because he could not present himself well at the interview.

An interview is a partnership where both the interviewer as well as the interviewee should be sincere in their efforts to make it a success.

Usually, an interview confirms the impression gained from the written application. But sometimes the 'face-to-encounter' produces a different impression, good or bad, based on the participation in the interview process.

There is no particular level of preparation for an interview. It will depend on the type of job and your state of mind to face such an interview.

Thus the need for a good preparation for an interview speaks for itself.

How do you Present Yourself?

An interview is an important occasion. And you are expected to dress appropriately to the occasion. Dress well, not too gaudy and not too simple. Dress very modestly and tidily to suit the job you have applied for, with a good hair style that suit your personality. Remember, if you are dressed too casual then the interviewer may be forced on a conclusion that the candidate may be even casual in other things too.

Sometime it is so disheartening to learn that some candidates who turn up an interview either they don't really want the job or they are not sure and make a half-hearted attempt. No, you must be really serious about the job you have applied for and you must be very confident and mentally prepared to face such an interview.

You must have your referees, certificates ready all the time.

Anxious Moments while Waiting

Waiting always makes a person impatient. It makes you quite tense especially when you are waiting for your turn for an interview, which is going to decide your future.

Generally, candidates are given staggered timings for their interviews to avoid their long waiting. However, you should expect a reasonable waiting in the waiting place before you are called in for interview.

Make sure you reach the place of interview well on time and never be late. If you are late, it will create an impression that you are a bad time-keeper.

But in case you are unable to reach at the given time due to certain reasons beyond your control, you should inform the authorities well in time so that they may give you another chance.

Appear 'bright and fresh' at the beginning of the interview. Whether your turn comes first, in middle or at the end, you will be right in expecting the interviewer to be considerate in putting the questions across to you and to give a patient hearing to your answers.

There may or may not be other candidates waiting for their turn for interview. And their actions and reactions may unnecessarily worry you in many ways.

If you are waiting alone, the loneliness may make you quite nervous. If others are also waiting, you may get jittery and confused listening to their gossip and apparent confidence.

Some of the candidates discuss a lot of things including their experiences and show off their confidence to face the interview as if everything about the interview is already known to them. This may be a way to cover up their weakness. Similarly, you may find those waiting may look gloomy about the whole thing. Such things should not matter to you at all as long as you are confident in yourself.

Under such circumstances the best thing for you will be to keep cool and keep your mind active and alert. Run over the likely questions you expect to come up during your interview and try to find suitable answers for them. This will help you to answer to questions put across to you by the interviewer from your fresh memory and you need not wait to find an answer.

Never learn answers for the likely questions. This will only harm you in certain situations. Your facts, ideas should be expressed in your own words as it comes to your mind.

At the same time, you must be mentally prepared for any kind of unexpected questions or turn of events like sudden change of topics, so that you are not surprised and shocked at such a thing if at all happens.

It is quite natural to be inquisitive about what is going on inside the interview room and reaction of the candidates coming after their interview. Let such things not bother you much and get carried away by their comments. You never know, they may be good actors, better than you.

Another thing that may bother you is when you know that you are one of last few candidates for the interview. You may be worried thinking that others ahead of you would have made the interviewer quite tired and irritated after such a long interview schedule and that you are going to have a tough time ahead. This is not true. An interviewer is a well experienced person, who knows such things pretty well and will be fully prepared.

Normally, calls for interviews to the short listed candidates may be sent in an alphabetical order, based on the CV (their qualification and experience etc.) or at random as the applications are received. Therefore, the order for interview should not up set you in any way. It all depended on you, how you perform and the impression you create at the interview.

At the Interview

When your turn comes, enter the interview room with all your certificates and testimonials in your hand in a good file or folder, with a cool mind, full confidence and a cheerful face.

As you enter the room, wish the interviewer/ the interviewing board. Do not sit until you are offered a seat. While sitting down there may be a few moments before the interviewer begins with you. During these few moments do not look round the room. Sit erect and focus on the interviewer and be alert to receive any questions.

The interviewer may ask you a few things on your CV, things which he wants to know or clarify. You must answer them briefly to the point. You may offer any supplementary information you think may help.

He may also ask you some points of confidential nature he has gathered on you. Do not get upset or react to the questions he asks you. Answer them politely and always with a pleasing look.

The initial questions will give you some idea about the interviewer and his way of putting things and will also give you an idea how you should respond to his questions.

The interviewer already knows about your qualification from your CV. Now he needs to probe to discover the *real person* in you, your strength and weakness.

Further questioning will be to assess you on your ability, your knowledge, on your work experience, your personal qualities and other interests and will depend on the nature of your application.

A question on your 'ambition' is quite common. Don't be afraid to disclose your ambitions in life. A reasonable ambition will reinforce the candidate's willingness to work hard to achieve his ambition.

When you come up for the interview you probably have some idea about various questions that are likely to be asked. But at times, he may ask you some personal questions, which you may feel offended. Such questions though personal, are required to assess some of your personal qualities. Well, you need to answer them patiently.

The type questions and the style of questioning may be different. But that should not worry you in any way.

Whenever a question is asked if you have not followed it correctly you should ask the interviewer to repeat the question and then start answering.

Question and answer are stimulus and response. The right question will provoke an informative answer.

At times, the interviewer may ask you some questions on some imaginary situation. Answer them carefully and in brief as to how you will react in such a situation.

Sometime question may switch suddenly from one topic to another. A sudden change of topic catches nearly everyone off guard, so an interviewer may use this method if he suspects that there are some matters you wish to avoid or to cover up. Take a little time to reconcile to the situation and answer them.

An interview situation is more fitting for an 'extrovert' than an introvert. But at the same time, an introvert will be asking for trouble if he/she left everything to the interviewer to discover his qualities. Remember, an interview is a partnership activity and even an introvert should put in the best.

You must show enthusiasm throughout your interview. Let the tension about the outcome not worry you.

Interview for a Change of Job

When appearing for an interview for a change of job, you will have more experience and are expected to know more than a fresh candidate. Obviously you can expect a good questioning and it will depend on the type and duration of your earlier employment.

The likely questions among others will include, questions about your last job, the reason for leaving that job, reason for dismissal from your previous company (if you were dismissed) and your reasons for taking up this job.

Whatever good reasons you may have, too many moves in a short period will cause concern.

Your answers must be quite convincing or else the interviewer will be forced to form his own opinion about your career history.

Some likely Questions at the Interview

Initial set of questions may be about your education, qualification, work experience and family background.

Why did you apply for this job?
What are your so called achievements in your life?
What are your strong points?
What are your weak points?
Do you really enjoy your work?
What does 'job satisfaction' mean to you?
What really motivates you?
What was the exact nature of the work in your last job?
How did you hear about us?
Do you really want this job?
What are your ambitions?

How do you use your spare time?
Do you have any cultural interests?
There may be questions about your hobbies, like,
Why do you read?
Do you read for information or pleasure?
What are your abilities and aptitudes?
How well you get along with others?
Do you possess leadership qualities?
How do you react in situations of strain?
Are you trust worthy?
Do you possess initiative?
Do you give up easily?
Why have you quit your previous job? (Your reasons must be quite convincing)
Why so many (so few) changes?
Did all the changes lead to greater experience, more responsibility, promotion?
How long did you stay in your last job?
There may be some personal questions.
There may be some hypothetical questions.

Why many people don't make the Grade at the Interview?

With heavy unemployment rate, the employers have a chance to pick and choose the best candidates to fill in their job vacancies. There is no dearth of applicants. At times, the grade of the applicants is so good that they find it too hard to select the best of the lot. Under such circumstances it is always advisable to carry out an analysis to find out what could have caused for not being considered for the job you had applied for.

Some of the points that had led to such a situation could be:

- Your qualifications do not match the job requirements.
- Your experience may be quite inadequate or may be the experience in a different field altogether.
- You may not possess the personal qualities the employer is looking for.

- Your frequent change of jobs and your reasons may not be quite convincing and the employer is not sure of your continuing in the job.
- You may have difficult terms and conditions, which may not be acceptable to the employer.
- Your poor performance at the interview.
- Luck may not be in your favor.

Some Helpful Tips

- Prepare well to present your case in an interview.
- Preferably try and do a career counseling.
- Be confident. But never appear over confident or boastful.
- Develop a good communication skill.
- Dress appropriately to the occasion.
- Ask yourself as to what impression you want to create and what impression you do create while presenting yourself?
- Appear 'bright and fresh' at the beginning of the interview and try to maintain the same till the end.
- Be prepared with all the basic facts about your education, qualification, experience, other interests that an interviewer is most likely to ask.
- Think before you speak.. Be cautious in your approach. At the same time you should not be too cautious that you take considerable time to answer every time causing irritation to the interviewer.
- Spontaneous, straight forward answers given without hesitation carry conviction, particularly if they are backed up by a frank, open manner.
- Give a convincing reply to 'Why did you apply for this job?'
- Avoid any unnecessary mannerism.
- Hypothetical questions must be answered with care. The situation described may be very similar to a real one. Answer them by explaining the general principles you would apply to such a problem.
- Ambitions are revealing because they show some degree of self-assessment. Have some realistic ambitions in life. Realistic ambitions will reinforce the candidate's willingness to work to achieve his/her ambition.

- Never get offended at some of the personal questions. Such questions though personal, are required to assess some of your personal qualities. Therefore, answer them patiently.
- And finally, there is always an element of luck in being successful at an interview and therefore, hope for the best.

This may be your first job interview and there is nothing much to regret. It has given you some experience for a second interview. But remember, no two interviews will be the same.

It gives you a chance to identify your weakness and helps you to improve upon them before you attempt for another job interview.

It helps you to correct your ideas about the labour market and set your high hopes and expectations.

You would have gained a lot from the interaction with a number of people at the time of your first interview. It increases your self-confidence.

****

New Work Culture

The Need: What makes "Online World" so powerful is its amazing worldwide reach, its ability to create huge social networks in minutes, and to put you in touch with thousands of people in fractions of seconds. Growth in the field of science and technology has also made the Online World very powerful, which has changed our life style altogether.

But if you look a few decades back, the technology, job recruitment, working environment and the employer / employee relationship were not the same as what we see and experience today.

In order to keep up with the fast-growing technology development, there have been tremendous changes in every field of activity of any commercial organization. Obviously, we need to match up with the overall developments that are taking place today.

The QR of the employees has gone up considerably. Today, companies are looking for candidates with some added qualification in addition to their basic qualification. Overseas Recruitments are done thus making their Work Force multilingual and multi cultured.

So, it's time to adopt a new 'Work Culture' that will improve the working environment and increase their working efficiency.

Work Culture

It is a combination of qualities of an organization and its employees that arise from what is generally regarded as appropriate ways to think and act.

Work occupies most of our life, if you think about it...officially you are supposed to work for 8 hrs per day to be considered full time. But, people work differently in different countries depending on the culture.

Company Culture

It is the personality of a company. It defines the environment in which employees work. Company culture includes a variety of elements, including work environment, company mission, value, ethics, expectations, and goals.

For example, some companies have a team-based culture with employee participation on all levels, while others have a more traditional and formal management style.

Company Culture is important to employees, because workers are more likely to enjoy their time in the workplace when they fit in with the 'Company Culture'. Employees tend to enjoy work when their needs and values are consistent with those in the workplace.

For example, if you prefer to work independently, but work for a company that emphasizes teamwork (or has shared office spaces), you are likely to be less happy and less efficient.

When an employee fits in with the culture, they are also likely to want to work for that company for longer. Thus, employers can improve productivity and employee retention through a strong office culture. Accordingly, a new Work Culture is adopted to include the following factors:-

The Structure

The organizational structure itself is being changed to suit the present-day demands. The change from a 'hierarchy' based management structure to a 'horizontal' management structure in the corporate sector, especially in the field of information technology, is a clear example of the rising needs.

Managerial system is revived and Managerial cadre equipped to take on the present-day challenges.

Specialized managerial courses are available to train the old and the new alike. There are various Managerial Development Programs organized by institutions to improve the managerial quality.

Job Satisfaction

Job Satisfaction in any field may be defined as a positive emotional state resulting from the appraisal of what derives from one's own job experience. It reflects how well the job meets an employee's basic expectations.

If an employee feels that he works very hard but is given a raw deal by the management and peer-group, he will be dissatisfied. On the other hand, if he feels that he is treated well, and has an opportunity to do the work of his choice, he will have a positive attitude towards his work and his productivity will increase.

Relationship

Today, one cannot do things on one's own; it is essential to evolve a system to involve the efforts of everybody in the team, each pulling their weight and contributing their share. It is vital therefore to bond with coworkers, and build relationship with people we work with.

It is an art to carry yourself with greater ease and to get the support of your coworkers.

Nip any misunderstandings and disputes in the bud. It's easily said but difficult to achieve. It needs diplomacy and tact. It means facing issues without being confrontationist. Be a good 'listener'.

Develop an ability to imagine and share another person's feelings, experience etc. Try and understand the reason why the other person is behaving the way they are. If you can understand the 'whys' and 'wherefores', you can always find a solution.

If you don't like a job or don't do it, how can you expect others to do it, or do it with enthusiasm?

Be Professional and Patently Efficient

Your own performance should be superlative. Approach your work with exemplary professionalism. Do whatever is given to you and you will find that everybody is beginning to tackle his or her jobs. If you don't like a job or don't do it, how can you expect others in your team to do it?

Take on what you can chew

Doing more than you need to can be a great motivator. It will get you the admiration of your fellow workers, especially when you lend a shoulder to their wheels. This will get you any help when you are in need. Take care not to bite off things more than you can possibly chew. Not been able to deliver the goods can make you a laughing stock in the office.

No Gossiping

It's a wrong notion that only women gossip. Well, men also get into gossip. And it's a hard habit to break. Generally gossiping can cause problems, as it is a way to build networking and allies.

By indulging in gossip you are undermining your own reputation and the trust people place in you. And therefore, it's better to turn away from gossip. Another point is that if you are seen indulged in gossiping, you will find that people will start avoiding you; because they can never be sure of you talking behind their backs.

Open Your Talk Channels

Always talk to your coworkers you can. Even a word in passing is loads better than no word at all. Ask a question or two, they could be related to work or family, the communication lines should always be open.

This habit builds trust and builds teams. It adds to learning. If you share your knowledge, your allies will share knowledge with you and this will invigorate your career. Remember, if you don't want to learn, knowledge will be out sourced, as everything is today, and you will become redundant.

Good Communication Skill

The need for a good interpersonal skill within the organization and corporate levels and with outside agencies has become a must for a better output in the present scenario. Further, a good interpersonal skill and a good communication skill at the middle, senior and top management levels are the call of the day. A good communication skill can definitely improve the personal relationship within the organization.

Remember, a healthy 'Work Culture' leads to satisfied employees and an increased productivity.

So, it is very important to understand the importance of new 'Work Culture' and try to fit into that Work Culture. Secondly, based on your qualification and Dream Job that you are looking for, you must be able to find out the companies with the kind of 'Company Culture' that you are looking for and do your Job Search in such companies. And finally, most important thing, you must be able to fit in their 'Work Culture' so that you can enjoy a good career growth in that company.

****

Work Culture in IT

The new economy offers unprecedented opportunities for the hard-working and enterprising employees, particularly so in the information technology sector. The traditional reward system has undergone a sea-change in this information age.

In the case of companies in the field of information technology, *it is the job requirement that has made the changes in the working style and the work culture.*

The parameters such as salary, perks, stock options, profit-sharing, work environment, promotions, supervision, nature of work, peer-group acceptance etc. have different connotations for IT employees.

The Structure

Present-day IT jobs are characterized by a horizontal management structure, rather than a hierarchy based (vertical) one, especially in the startup companies.

Skill and Knowledge

Skill, rather than experience, is the hallmark of IT jobs. A fresh graduate with good knowledge of some IT area is paid more than an Executive in other fields with a decade-long experience.

The concept of rewards has undergone a sea-change in the Information Age. Skill, rather than experience, alone is considered a more relevant parameter for IT jobs.

Job Satisfaction

Info Tech jobs are somewhat different in respect of the traditional concepts of job satisfaction.

For a knowledge-based enterprise, job satisfaction must be viewed in the context of high salary-level, rapid rate of obsolescence, target based work-schedule, and a horizontal (rather than rigid hierarchy-based) management structure that characterizes a startup company.

Financial remuneration still remains one of the important criteria for job satisfaction. Employees with experience see pay as an indication of how the management views their contribution to their organization; if the pay is relatively poor, it indicates the management is not pleased with them; and they need to improve.

Working Environment

The right environment and working conditions influence job satisfaction of an IT employee.

They attach great importance to clean and attractive surroundings. They do not tolerate the dusty, noisy atmosphere prevailing in the conventional industries. They consider themselves as a class apart, and deserve nothing but the best. They would like to be surrounded by a 'computer geeks' and talk a computer-savvy-lingo quite different from that of others.

The usual 8-4 job concept is anathema to them. They would like to start with their 'key boards' at about 11 a.m. to be back home at mid-night. Sometimes, they will even sleep in the office itself and there must be provision for that.

They are not amenable, rather unwilling to be influenced or controlled, to attendance registers, and punch cards, which are now replaced by *'Targets'*.

The daylong information generated in India will be down loaded at night through the international gateway to the U.S., when it will be daytime there. Thus work is done and targets met on 24-hours-a-day basis for the global MNCs.

Supervision

Studies on the organizational behavior consider 'Supervision' as one of the factors influencing job satisfaction. If a supervisor takes considerable interest in the welfare of the employee, it promotes improved job satisfaction. The supervisor's standing does make a difference to the info-tech employees, who have a better opportunity to learn new skills and techniques under an expert.

Promotions

The rewards in IT jobs are performance driven. A senior manager is just as much as a junior executive.

Successive promotions will lead to better pay, perks and status within the organizations. It need not be increased 'power' or authority.

Perform or Quit

The underlying mantra in IT career is "Perform or Quit". The computer and telecommunication industries are subject to rapid obsolescence, the kind of which no other industry has witnessed. Things change by the year, or even within a few months' time. Therefore, one has to keep up-dated all the time. This is the main reason why young people are preferred for IT jobs.

Stock Options

The IT Age has accelerated the concept of stock ownership ie. Employees Stock Option Plan (ESOP). Employees are allowed to purchase shares at a concessional price, or some per cent of shares given free. This is because the fortunes of the companies in the share market ultimately depend on employee performance and their productivity. An employee may feel that he is also a part owner of the company and this feeling is bound to improve his performance and productivity. Eligibility for stock ownership may depend on the number of years of service and their relative position in their companies.

A recent feature of managerial motivation in IT companies is the grant of stock option. Many present-day managers are attracted by such offers.

Profit-sharing Plans

Traditionally, profit-sharing plans have sometimes ended in a fiasco because of improper relationship between the management and their employees. But the advent of Information Age has changed such misgivings. The old ways have to go into the New Economy.

The 'Knowledge-Trade' is not possible without active involvement of the employees, who are highly educated and 'knowledgeable'. They are not mere employees; they are 'knowledge workers'; they need to be treated on a different plane. And this approach must be sophisticated.

Company's work out their own 'profit-sharing' plans for their employees at all levels.

Frequent Change of Companies

Frequent change of companies by the IT professionals is the most experienced in the corporate history. They tend to hop from one company to another without any qualms or feeling of guilt.

IT companies have realized that people sometimes join them for a lesser pay package for an altogether reason. Such entrants are motivated by the fact that they would be able to learn a new language or have access to the latest software package for which they would have to pay a huge amount outside. And they view such job opportunities to update their knowledge to be used to their own advantage from the point of view of a lucrative foreign job.

The Guiding Principle

'Let us survive collectively rather than in isolation' seems to be the motto and guiding principle especially for a 'start-up IT Company'.

Thus, the management of the IT companies is inclined to treat the IT professionals as a part of them. Because they know that the success of their companies lie in retaining them (IT professional) by providing a high degree of job satisfaction and even by allowing them to share a part of their profit.

****

Careers in IT– Risk Factors

It's a universal law that everything in this nature/ world must be balanced. So is the case with the IT industry. While IT industry has better points as one could possibly think off in the industry, it also has the negative side to balance its better side. They could be better described as 'Risk Factors' in IT industry.

Work Pressure

Several new techniques, hardware, software and languages are in the market and it is almost impossible to master all of them in a life-time. If a person chooses an area that he not very confident of, his professional life may be hell.

There is no point in choosing a highly paid, lucrative job, if the demands associated with it cannot be met with. Nobody is going to pamper you with sky-high salary, if you cannot live up to the expectations of the management.

Actually, a job one can accomplish with a high degree of confidence level, can be more satisfying than a highly paid one, where one feels like a misfit all the time.

One can not afford to be choosy about the field of your career in IT industry. *You must have a will to learn and a will to work; it's another key to your success.*

Quite an Unpredictable Profession

At the rate of technological advance as we witness today, the growth rate in the field of IT is quite unpredictable. And so is about the career opportunities IT industry can offer.

In spite of your best efforts and willingness to update yourself, at one point of time you will feel quite tired to keep updated. And even at the managerial level, they require managers always updated with the latest technology who can support and control the workforce under them. Thus your job security at managerial level is also unpredictable.

Personal Qualities can *Make or Break your Career*

Your personal qualities have great bearing on your success in IT industry. You must be adaptable to the new and the changing environment and the new work culture that is being followed in the IT industry.

Self-confidence, determination, initiative, drive, cooperation and good interaction with your colleagues, dependability, trust worthiness etc are some of the personal qualities that can take you a long way.

Losing Interest over a Period of Time

Various courses in the IT sector today require time and are also very expensive. It's the general tendency to do the minimum required courses to get into a career in IT industry. And you always plan to update yourself as you continue to work. In the initial years of your career you may be able to cope up your working schedule and your extra effort to do additional courses for updating yourself. But in the later years, you may be so much involved in your work, especially so when it is target based, you may find it difficult to spare time for pursuing your career prospects.

Further, the time and effort required for updating yourself may be so much that you may loose your interest in doing so at one particular point of time and you may be willing to settle with what you have achieved so far.

Job Security

Job security in the IT industry is far less. If you have not made the grade, you may be 'fired' at any time.

While the IT industry has generated tremendous career opportunities for qualified and young IT professionals, the quest for high profile jobs with good returns has created stiff competition for the jobs in the IT industries.

The QR (qualitative requirement) of various IT professions are increasing day by day. And IT companies, in spite of their high tech selection process, often do not get professionals with their desired professional skill level and look for a better replacement.

As an employee you must get adjusted with the working system of your company and try to be a part of their team. Or else it can even cost your career in that company.

And thus, IT industry is a field, which has everything you are looking forward to. At the same time, it is the most unpredictable industry about its growth, future and career opportunities. All the same it's an area where the young generation has a great future ahead of them provided they have **a *'Will to learn, Will to work and Work harder'*.**

****

Search for your Dream Job

Having fulfilled all the requirements it's time that you start searching for your Dream Job.

New to Job Search?

Here are some Tips to find your Dream Job. If you are new to job search, this post will help you through the process of looking for your Dream Job. Just read through this and follow the steps. It will certainly help to find your Dream Job.

Step 1: Find out about jobs

Step 2: Write or update your CV

Step 3: Check your social media profile

Step 4: Search and apply for suitable jobs

Step 5: Prepare and practice for job interviews

Step 6: Attend job interviews

Step 7: Get a job offer.

Step 1: Find out about jobs: Research the types of jobs you are looking for. Things to consider include:

- What job opportunities are available in your region?
- What skills or qualifications do these jobs require, and how do these match your own?
- What organizations have the jobs you are looking for? Use their websites to research those organizations.
- Jobs database – look up jobs to find out their entry requirements and your job chances

Step 2: Write or update your CV: This is a very important document which you will be updating whenever required, in your career.

- Gather information for your CV
- Use your research to make a list of the skills you have that match the job requirements.
- Record examples of how you have demonstrated these skills.
- Find referees who can vouch for your skills and good character.
- Figure out your skills - how to identify what skills you have.

Write your CV - Writing your CV is a chance to think about what someone reading it, an employer, will think about what you can do in a job.

- CVs - getting started
- CV styles -find out what style of CV would suit you best.

Step 3: Check your social media profile: Regard your social media profile as part of your application as employers may use it to find out about you. Be sensible about the information you post online, or change your settings so your profile is not publicly available.

Step 4: Search and apply for suitable jobs - an important step

- Searching for job vacancies
- Use a variety of search methods to find more work opportunities.
- How to find out about job vacancies
- Job vacancy and recruitment agency website links
- Applying for jobs

Make sure you:

- Keep a record of your applications

- Keep your referees informed about the jobs you apply for
- Send a cover letter and CV.
- CV and cover letter templates – use our templates to help you write your cover letters
- Job vacancy and recruitment agency website links.

Step 5: Prepare and practice for job interviews:

- Think about what kind of questions an employer might ask you.
- Write down your answers to possible questions.
- Practice answering interview questions with friends.
- Use your research to write down some questions you can ask employers at interviews.
- Preparing for a job interview
- Tips for answering interview questions
- Questions you can ask at an interview

Step 6: Attend job interviews: No matter how hard you try, it is likely that not every application will gain you a job interview. So congratulate yourself when you are offered an interview!

Make sure you:

- Arrive early for the interview
- Have your list of questions you want to ask and copies of your CV and the job information
- Know why you want the job
- Dress neatly and in clothing that would be appropriate for the job.
- Work and Income website - find out about getting a clothing grant through the Transition to Work programme.
- Dress for Success website - helps disadvantaged women find appropriate business clothes for job interviews

Step 7: Get a job offer: If you are offered a job, your employer will usually make a verbal offer first. They will then send you an employment agreement, which will outline the details of your employment.

Before you sign an employment agreement, study the details, and get advice if you need it.

Dealing with job offers and negotiating employment contracts - more tips and advice.

Job Search – Why Go Online?

As mentioned in the section above, if you've used Facebook to connect with old friends, you already know how powerful a tool the Internet can be. But why is the Internet particularly useful for a job search? For quite a few reasons – including the following ones:

- You'll have access to job postings in all sectors of work, at all levels and pay grades, all over the world.

- You can search for jobs at any hour of the day or night, on any day of the week, whenever you have time.

- You'll gain practice with computer skills, which means you'll be beefing up your skill set as you search.

- Online interactions are lower-pressure than face-to-face ones, so it'll be easier to keep your composure

Tools will help you discover and browse career areas you might never have considered.

- Once you get used to the process, it's a whole lot easier than a traditional job search...

But the strongest argument for taking your job search online is that, once you get used to the process, it's a whole lot easier than a traditional job search. All you've got to do is type a few keywords into a job website's search box, and you're presented with pages and pages of jobs related to your specific interests. And once you register an account on a job-search site, you can save your searches and run them again with a click of a button – or even set up email alerts to let you know as soon as new openings that match your interests get posted. And all you've got to do is sit back and pick the ones you like.

Job Search – Before You Go Online

Preparation for an online job search doesn't take much – and in fact, it has a lot in common with preparation for a traditional job search. The first thing you must do is to make sure you've got your resume up to date, and formatted as a Word document, a PDF file and a plain text document. As you update your resume, take notice of the keywords you're using, and jot down some notes of the ones that seem most relevant to the types of jobs you're looking for.

These keywords can fall into several categories, each of which forms the answer to a certain type of question:

Who are you, in terms of your training, your qualifications and your job titles? For example, are you an air conditioning technician, a chemistry teacher or an administrative assistant?

What do you do, what can you do, and what do you want to do? For example, are you an expert in welding? Have you corrected legal documents? Do you like serving as a project manager?

What fields interest you, and which subfields particularly catch your interest? For example, are you just interested in healthcare in general, or in medical equipment sales? Are you only passionate about nonprofit public relations, or can you see yourself working in PR for other types of organizations as well?

Who do you want to work for, and how does this relate to your previous employers? For example, do you have experience at small companies but dream of working for a Fortune 500 employer? Have you worked for tech start-ups but want to branch out into launching other types of businesses?

Where do you want to work, geographically and environmentally? Are you limited to the East Coast, or specifically to the state of Maryland? Are you a city person, or are you open to rural work? Do you need a stable living situation, or can you travel freely?

Once you get used to the process, it's much easier than a traditional job search.

Although your resume may not answer all these questions, thinking about them will give you some solid starting points for putting together the list of keywords and search settings you'll use as you look for jobs online. If you find yourself having trouble generating keywords, there are other places you can go for help, too. Try asking your friends for their insights on your talents and passions. Ask a librarian, or a worker at a job center, for help describing the type of work you'd like to do. Or browse through some websites related to your area of work, and note down any keywords that catch your eye. Before long, you'll have a ready supply of terms to use when you start searching for jobs.

Select Right Sites for your Job Search

How do you decide which resources will fit your needs? Try asking yourself the following questions below as you scan a site.

What does the site offer? Some sites offer only job listings, while others also offer networking opportunities, discussion groups, articles and newsletters with job-search tips, and even lists of trade associations you can contact for more info on certain professions.

There's no point registering for a site that only lists a few new jobs per week.

How frequently are the listings updated? Most of the largest job websites are drowning in hundreds or thousands of new posts every day – but there's probably no point registering for a site that only gets a few new job listings per week. If you see a lot of listings that are at least 30 days old, or only a few from the current week, that site probably isn't worth your time.

Who runs the site? You can easily find this out by clicking the "About Us" link that's at the very top or bottom of almost every major job website. If you don't recognize the company that runs the site, plug their name into Google and find out a little more about them. While many companies are perfectly legitimate, others may not be as trustworthy or helpful.

Do the admins respond to messages? If you're going to be spending a lot of time on a given site, you'll want to make sure the customer support staff are eager to help in case of a problem. Try firing off a quick email or message to them, asking any of the questions above, or just saying you want to check on their responsiveness. If they don't get back to you, you can save yourself a lot of trouble by moving on to other sites.

What's the privacy policy say? Some job-search websites make money on the side by selling members' information to advertisers and other shady companies, so be sure to take a look at each site's privacy policy to make sure your information won't be shared with any third parties. If the policy doesn't guarantee this, there are plenty more sites you can use.

If there's a fee, is it worth it? Quite a few job-search sites are free for basic use, but some charge a fee for advanced features like networking and high-volume messaging. Depending on your situation, some of the paid features may be worth your money – but never trust a site that charges you, or makes you register, just to take a peek. Any site that's trustworthy will at least give you a look for free.

Remember, only you can decide whether a site and its resources meet your needs. Asking friends, family members, colleagues, and even others in your job transition group (if you're a member of one) will help you create a list of starting points for your search – and it might also cross some sites off your list as others relate problems they've had. So go ahead and exchange ideas with others as you begin your search – but keep in mind that these are just suggestions. If they don't work out, you can always jump on Google, track down some other promising sites, and branch out on your own.

How to Create a Healthy Work Culture?

Here are the characteristics of a healthy Work Culture:-

Healthy work culture leads to satisfied employees and an increased productivity.

Employees must be cordial with each other. One must respect his fellow worker. Backbiting is considered strictly unprofessional and must be avoided for a healthy work culture. One gains nothing out of conflicts and nasty politics at work.

Each employee should be treated as one. Partiality leads to demotivated employees and eventually an unhealthy work culture. Employees should be judged only by their work and nothing else. Personal relationships should take a backseat at the workplace. Don't favor anyone just because he is your relative.

Appreciating the top performers is important. Praise the employees to expect good work from them every time. Give them a pat on their back. Let them feel indispensable for their organization. Don't criticize the ones who have not performed well, instead ask them to pull up their socks for the next time. Give them one more opportunity rather than firing them immediately.

Encourage discussions at the workplace. Employees must discuss issues among themselves to reach to better conclusions. Each one should have the liberty to express his views. The team leaders and managers must interact with the subordinates frequently. Transparency is essential at all levels for better relationships among employees and a healthy work culture. Manipulating information and data tampering is a strict no no at the workplace. Let information flow in its desired form.

Organization must have employee friendly policies and practical guidelines. Expecting an employee to work till late night on his birthday is simply impractical. Rules and regulations should be made to benefit the employees. Employees must maintain the decorum of the organization. Discipline is important at the workplace.

The "Hitler approach" does not fit in the current scenario. Bosses should be more like mentors to the employees. The team leaders should be a source of inspiration for the subordinates. The superiors are expected to provide a sense of direction to the employees and guide them whenever needed. The team members should have an easy access to their boss's cabin.

Promote team building activities to bind the employees together. Conduct training programs, workshops, seminars and presentations to upgrade the existing skills of the employees. Prepare them for the tough times. They should be ready under any odd circumstances or change in the work culture.

****

How to become
A Successful Professional?

Success may be defined in different ways, but being an informed and dedicated employee, a strong leader, and an honest person can all make a big difference in making you a successful professional in any career.

No matter how you define your goals or what field you working, strengthening your professional skills, building professional relationships, and being a self-motivated professional can help you achieve success and satisfaction in your career.

To sum up, given below are some tips to become a successful Professional.

Developing your skills
- Strengthen your skills
- Exercise your communication skill
- Work on interpersonal skills
- Learn Leadership skills

Building Professional Relationship
- Offer help without being asked
- Show appreciation at every step
- Take an interest in coworkers/ employees
- Practice Networking

Taking Control of your Career
- Take responsibility for your actions
- Be self –motivated
- Learn to ask
- Make Specific, Measurable, Achievable, Results-focused, and Time-bound (S.M.A.R.T.) goals.

By following above tips, your career will take you to new heights of which you will be proud of.

Professionalism is all about conduct, core values and ethics at workplace. In order to be a successful professional, one needs to have strong work ethics because it is a quality favored at the work place. Such employees are valued in every organization and it is very common for companies to run a few extra miles to make their professional force stay in the organization. Hence, apply careful thought into your own work philosophies that can help you advance in your career.

Final Tips

Here are the TEN Commandments / Simple Qualities one should follow. They will help you to become a Successful Professional.

1. Be authentic: Be yourself. Let the results of your life reflect your readiness to express your personal freedoms.

2. Be truthful: There is nothing of greater significance to offer your life or business than honesty.

3. Challenge yourself: In order to make the most of your life and career, challenge yourself. You cannot fulfill even a fraction of your dreams by sticking to the comfortable and secure.

4. Put love first: The most significant people in your life are those who genuinely feel for and worry about you.

5. Be thoughtful: Treat all of those you interact with, with a sense of dignity and value.

6. Be a good human being: Be mindful of others in the ways you expect others to be mindful of you.

7. Practice patience: Knowing the difference between patience and waiting is key to a successful life and career. Patience is not about waiting. Waiting is action-less.

8. Live your dreams: Do not just follow your dreams, live them. Make each wish a manifested destiny. Work to make your dreams reality, with consistency, precision and commitment.

9. Have a grateful Heart: When you have a grateful   heart, your positive emotions become stronger, decreasing the   negative emotional experiences of   envy, victimization and jealousy.

10. Remain Humble: Commit to working quietly and   allowing your success to do the talking. Humility is based   in   internal reflection.

About the Author

George Maliakal has a passion for writing. Whether, while he was in the army or even after his premature retirement after 20 years, in spite of his hectic activities, he always found time to write on any topics that came to my mind. The rich life experience he has had throughout his life, also gave him lot of inspiration for writing.

His recent blog topics on 'Job Search' have been his favorite topics to help people searching for some jobs and help them to build up a good career for themselves.

"Towards Success- Become A Successful Professional",his recent book, is an 'All in One solution' for the Personal and Career Growth of young and old alike. It explains everything that you need to develop and practice as you grow, till you attain your goal of becoming a Successful Professional

To 'be a published author' was one among his endless dreams, which he realized very recently. Some of his written works

Fiction, non-fiction, reference book and many photo books were published very recently and they are listed by amzon.com, Itunes.apple.com and by other agencies for global marketing.

He has a unique personality with which he realizes his 'Endless Dreams'. He is very creative with innovative thoughts and has his own style of writing. At 73 plus, even with his multiple ailments, he is still very active and is planning to publish some more of his recent works shortly.

His major hobbies are Photography, Numismatics, Philately and pets. His YouTube channel with 197 videos enjoys a viewership from over 220 countries across the world. He has travelled extensively in India and also visited some countries abroad.

****

www.ingramcontent.com/pod-product-compliance
Lightning Source LLC
Chambersburg PA
CBHW050458290526
45786CB00006B/2342